OECD/G20 Base Erosion and Profit Shifting Project

Neutralising the Effects of Hybrid Mismatch Arrangements

OECD
BETTER POLICIES FOR BETTER LIVES

This document and any map included herein are without prejudice to the status of or sovereignty over any territory, to the delimitation of international frontiers and boundaries and to the name of any territory, city or area.

Please cite this publication as:
OECD (2014), *Neutralising the Effects of Hybrid Mismatch Arrangements*, OECD/G20 Base Erosion and Profit Shifting Project, OECD Publishing.
http://dx.doi.org/10.1787/9789264218819-en

ISBN 978-92-64-21879-6 (print)
ISBN 978-92-64-21881-9 (PDF)

Series: OECD/G20 Base Erosion and Profit Shifting Project
ISSN 2313-2604 (print)
ISSN 2313-2612 (online)

Photo credits: Cover © archerix / Fotolia.

Corrigenda to OECD publications may be found on line at: *www.oecd.org/about/publishing/corrigenda.htm*.

Foreword

Addressing base erosion and profit shifting (BEPS) is a key priority of governments around the globe. In 2013, OECD and G20 countries, working together on an equal footing, adopted a 15-point Action Plan to address BEPS. The Action Plan aims to ensure that profits are taxed where economic activities generating the profits are performed and where value is created. It was agreed that addressing BEPS is critical for countries and must be done in a timely manner, not least to prevent the existing consensus-based international tax framework from unravelling, which would increase uncertainty for businesses at a time when cross-border investments are more necessary than ever. As a result, the Action Plan provides for 15 actions to be delivered by 2015, with a number of actions to be delivered in 2014.

The OECD Committee on Fiscal Affairs (CFA), bringing together 44 countries on an equal footing (all OECD members, OECD accession countries, and G20 countries), has adopted a first set of seven deliverables described in the Action Plan and due in 2014. This report is part of these deliverables and is an output of Action 2.

Developing countries and other non-OECD/non-G20 economies have been extensively consulted through regional and global fora meetings and their input has been fed into the work. Business representatives, trade unions, civil society organisations and academics have also been very involved through opportunities to comment on discussion drafts. These have generated more than 3 500 pages of comments and were discussed at five public consultation meetings and via three webcasts that attracted more than 10 000 viewers.

The first set of reports and recommendations, delivered in 2014, addresses seven of the actions in the BEPS Action Plan published in July 2013. Given the Action Plan's aim of providing comprehensive and coherent solutions to BEPS, the proposed measures, while agreed, are not yet formally finalised. They may be affected by some of the decisions to be taken with respect to the 2015 deliverables with which the 2014 deliverable will interact. They do reflect consensus, as of July 2014, on a number of solutions to put an end to BEPS.

The adoption of this first set of deliverables and the implementation of the relevant measures by national governments mean that: hybrid mismatches will be neutralised; treaty shopping and other forms of treaty abuse will be addressed; abuse of transfer pricing rules in the key area of intangibles will be greatly minimised; and country-by-country reporting will provide governments with information on the global allocation of the profits, economic activity and taxes of MNEs. Equally, OECD and G20 countries have agreed upon a report concluding that it is feasible to implement BEPS measures through a multilateral instrument. They have also advanced the work to fight harmful tax practices, in particular in the area of IP regimes and tax rulings. Finally, they have reached a common understanding of the challenges raised by the digital economy, which will now allow them to deepen their work in this area, one in which BEPS is exacerbated.

By its nature, BEPS requires co-ordinated responses. This is why countries are investing time and resources in developing shared solutions to common problems. At the same time, countries retain their sovereignty over tax matters and measures may be implemented in different countries in different ways, as long as they do not conflict with countries' international legal commitments.

Table of contents

Figures

Table

Abbreviations and acronyms

BEPS	Base erosion and profit shifting
CFA	Committee on Fiscal Affairs
CFC	Controlled foreign company
CIV	Collective investment vehicles
CRS	Common Reporting Standard (Standard for Automatic Exchange of Financial Account Information)
OECD	Organisation for Economic Co-operation and Development
TRACE	Treaty Relief and Compliance Enhancement
WP1	Working Party No.1 on Tax Conventions and Related Questions
WP11	Working Party No.11 on Aggressive Tax Planning

Executive summary

1. Hybrid mismatch arrangements can be used to achieve double non-taxation including long-term tax deferral. They reduce the collective tax base of countries around the world even if it may sometimes be difficult to determine which individual country has lost tax revenue. Action 2 of the BEPS Action Plan[1] therefore calls for the development of model treaty provisions and recommendations regarding the design of domestic rules to neutralise the effect of hybrid instruments and entities.

2. This Report sets out those recommendations in two parts. Part I provides recommendations for domestic rules to neutralise the effect of hybrid mismatch arrangements. Part II sets out recommended changes to the OECD Model Tax Convention[2] to deal with transparent entities, including hybrid entities, and addresses the interaction between the recommendations included in Part I and the provisions of the OECD Model Tax Convention.

3. The Report focuses on hybrid mismatch arrangements which were of the most concern to jurisdictions. Further consideration will be given to refining the rules if there is evidence that the rules are not effective in neutralising hybrid mismatch arrangements that are of concern to jurisdictions.

4. Once translated into domestic law and tax treaties, these recommendations and model provisions will neutralise mismatches and put an end to multiple deductions for a single expense, deductions in one country without corresponding taxation in another or the generation of multiple foreign tax credits for one amount of foreign tax paid.

5. The work will now turn to developing guidance, in the form of a Commentary which will explain how the rules would operate in practice, including via practical examples.

6. Furthermore there are a number of specific areas where the recommended domestic rules in Part I may need to be further refined. This is the case for certain capital market transactions (such as on-market stock lending and repos) and the rules on imported hybrid mismatches.

7. In addition, concerns were raised by a number of countries and by business in the consultation responses over the application of the rules to hybrid regulatory capital that is issued intra-group. These concerns need to be further explored in order to clarify whether a special treatment under the hybrid mismatch rules is justified. Finally, the Report will need to clarify whether or not income taxed under a controlled foreign company (CFC) regime should be treated as included in ordinary income for the purposes of this Report and the related language is in brackets. No consensus has yet been reached on these issues but discussion will continue with a view to reaching agreement and to publishing the outcome together with the Commentary no later than September 2015. Until work on these two issues has been completed and a consensus reached countries are free in their policy choices in these areas.

8. The work on the Commentary and on the outstanding issues will seek input from stakeholders (including the Financial Stability Board on hybrid regulatory capital) to ensure that the rules are clear, operational for both taxpayers and tax administrations and that they strike the right balance between compliance costs and neutralising the tax benefit derived from hybrid mismatch arrangements.

Summary of Part I

9. Part I sets out recommendations for domestic law to address mismatches in tax outcomes where they arise in respect of payments made under a hybrid financial instrument or payments made to or by a hybrid entity. It also considers the need for rules that address indirect mismatches that arise when the effects of a hybrid mismatch arrangement are imported into a third jurisdiction.

10. The Report sets out some general recommendations for changes to domestic law and also specific recommendations for hybrid mismatch rules designed to neutralise the tax effects of the arrangements referred to above. These hybrid mismatch rules are linking rules that seek to align the tax treatment of an instrument or entity with the tax outcomes in the counterparty jurisdiction but otherwise do not disturb the tax or commercial outcomes. To avoid double taxation and to ensure that the mismatch is eliminated even where not all the jurisdictions adopt the rules, the recommended rules are divided into a primary response and a defensive rule. The defensive rule only applies where there is no hybrid mismatch rule in the other jurisdiction or the rule is not applied to the entity or arrangement.

11. The rules recommended in this Report take into account a number of design principles including the need for comprehensive rules that operate automatically without requiring to establish which jurisdiction has lost tax

revenue under the arrangement and that seek to minimise compliance and administration costs for both taxpayers and tax administrations. The recommendations are intended to drive taxpayers towards less complicated and more transparent cross-border investment structures that are easier for jurisdictions to address with more orthodox tax policy tools. Also, there is an interaction with the other action item, particularly Action 3 (dealing with the design of CFC rules)[3] and Action 4 (looking at interest deductions)[4], on which further guidance will be required.

12. The Report recognises the importance of co-ordination in the implementation and application of the hybrid mismatch rules. Such co-ordination includes the sharing of information to help jurisdictions and taxpayers to identify the potential for mismatches and the response required under the hybrid mismatch rule.

13. Part I is divided into seven chapters:

- Chapter 1 defines what a hybrid mismatch arrangement is.
- Chapters 2 to 4 identify and define the hybrid mismatch arrangements targeted by this Report and make recommendations as to the way jurisdictions should respond to them.
- Chapter 5 sets out measures to be taken by jurisdictions in implementing the recommendations and the principles that have informed the design of the recommended domestic rules. Jurisdictions that implement these rules should do so in a way that is consistent with the design principles.
- Chapters 6 and 7 provide definitions of the key terms used in this Report. Common definitions have been included to ensure consistency in the application and scope of these recommendations and to supplement specific definitions within the recommendations themselves.

Summary of Recommendations in Part I

Specific changes to domestic law

14. Part I of the Report recommends specific changes to domestic law to achieve a better alignment between domestic and cross-border tax outcomes. In particular, this Report recommends:

- denial of a dividend exemption for the relief of economic double taxation in respect of deductible payments made under financial instruments;

- the introduction of measures to prevent hybrid transfers being used to duplicate credits for taxes withheld at source;
- improvements to controlled foreign company and other offshore investment regimes to bring the income of hybrid entities within the charge to taxation under the investor jurisdiction and the imposition of information reporting requirements on such intermediaries to facilitate the ability of offshore investors and tax administrations to apply such rules; and
- rules restricting the tax transparency of reverse hybrids that are members of a controlled group.

Hybrid mismatch rules

15. In addition to these specific recommendations on the tax treatment of entities and instruments, which are designed to prevent mismatches from arising, Action 2 calls for hybrid mismatch rules that adjust the tax outcomes in one jurisdiction to align them with the tax consequences in another. Action 2 states that these rules may include domestic law provisions that:

- deny a deduction for a payment that is also deductible in another jurisdiction;
- prevent exemption or non-recognition for payments that are deductible by the payer; and
- deny a deduction for a payment that is not includible in ordinary income by the recipient (and is not subject to taxation under CFC or similar rules).

16. Action 2 therefore calls for domestic rules targeting two types of payment:

- payments under a hybrid mismatch arrangement that are deductible under the rules of the payer jurisdiction and not included in the ordinary income of the payee or a related investor (deduction / no inclusion or D/NI outcomes); and
- payments under a hybrid mismatch arrangements that give rise to duplicate deductions for the same payment (double deduction or DD outcomes).

17. In order to avoid the risk of double taxation, Action 2 also calls for "guidance on the co-ordination or tie breaker rules where more than one country seeks to apply such rules to a transaction or structure." For this reason the rules recommended in this Report are organised in a hierarchy so

that a jurisdiction does not need to apply the hybrid mismatch rule where there is another rule operating in the counterparty jurisdiction that is sufficient to neutralise the mismatch. The Report recommends that every jurisdiction introduce all the recommended rules so that the effect of hybrid mismatch arrangement is neutralised even if the counterparty jurisdiction does not have effective hybrid mismatch rules.

(a) D/NI outcomes

18. Both payments made under hybrid financial instruments and payments made by hybrid entities can give rise to D/NI outcomes. In respect of such hybrid mismatch arrangements this Report recommends that the response should be to deny the deduction in the payer's jurisdiction. In the event the payer jurisdiction does not respond to the mismatch this Report recommends the jurisdictions adopt a defensive rule that would require the payment to be included as ordinary income in the payee's jurisdiction. Recommendations for hybrid mismatch rules neutralising D/NI outcomes are set out in Chapter 2.

(b) DD outcomes

19. As well as producing D/NI outcomes, payments made by hybrid entities can, in certain circumstances, also give rise to DD outcomes. In respect of such payments this Report recommends that the primary response should be to deny the duplicate deduction in the parent jurisdiction. A defensive rule, that would require the deduction to be denied in the payer jurisdiction, would only apply in the event the parent jurisdiction did not adopt the primary response. Recommendations for hybrid mismatch rules neutralising DD outcomes are set out in Chapter 3.

(c) Indirect D/NI outcomes

20. Once a hybrid mismatch arrangement has been entered into between two jurisdictions without effective hybrid mismatch rules, it is a relatively simple matter to shift the effect of that mismatch into a third jurisdiction (through the use of an ordinary loan, for example). Therefore in order to protect the integrity of the recommendations, this Report further recommends that a payer jurisdiction deny a deduction for a payment where the payee sets the payment off against expenditure under a hybrid mismatch arrangement (i.e. the payment is made under an imported mismatch arrangement that results in an indirect D/NI outcome). Recommendations for hybrid mismatch rules neutralising indirect D/NI outcomes are set out in Chapter 4.

(d) Scope

21. Overly broad hybrid mismatch rules may be difficult to apply and administer. Accordingly, each hybrid mismatch rule has its own defined scope, which is designed to achieve an overall balance between a rule that is comprehensive, targeted and administrable.

22. Table 1 provides a general overview of the recommendations in this Report.

Table 1. General overview of the recommendations

Mismatch	Arrangement	Specific recommendations on improvements to domestic law	Recommended hybrid mismatch rule		
			Response	Defensive rule	Scope
D/NI	Hybrid financial instrument	No dividend exemption for deductible payments Proportionate limitation of withholding tax credits	Deny payer deduction	Include as ordinary income	Related parties and structured arrangements
	Disregarded payment made by a hybrid		Deny payer deduction	Include as ordinary income	Controlled group and structured arrangements
	Payment made to a reverse hybrid	Improvements to offshore investment regime Restricting tax transparency of intermediate entities where non-resident investors treat the entity as opaque	Deny payer deduction	-	Controlled group and structured arrangements
DD	Deductible payment made by a hybrid		Deny parent deduction	Deny payer deduction	No limitation on response, defensive rule applies to controlled group and structured arrangements
	Deductible payment made by dual resident		Deny resident deduction	-	No limitation on response.
Indirect D/NI	Imported mismatch arrangements		Deny payer deduction	-	Members of controlled group and structured arrangements

Summary of Part II

23. Part II complements Part I and deals with the parts of Action 2 that indicate that the outputs of the work on Action 2 may include "changes to the OECD Model Tax Convention to ensure that hybrid instruments and entities (as well as dual resident entities) are not used to obtain the benefits of treaties unduly" and that stress that "[s]pecial attention should be given to the interaction between possible changes to domestic law and the provisions of the OECD Model Tax Convention."[5]

24. Part II is divided into three chapters:

- Chapter 8 examines issues related to dual-resident entities with a view to ensuring that dual-resident entities are not used to obtain the benefits of treaties unduly.
- Chapter 9 examines issues related to transparent entities and proposes a new treaty provision dealing with such entities and a detailed Commentary on that provision.
- Chapter 10 discusses the interaction between the recommendations in Part I and the provisions of the OECD Model Tax Convention.

Chapter 8 - Dual-resident companies

25. Chapter 8 of Part II addresses the part of Action 2 that refers expressly to possible changes to the OECD Model Tax Convention to ensure that dual resident entities are not used to obtain the benefits of treaties unduly. The change to Art. 4(3) of the OECD Model Tax Convention[6] that is recommended as part of the work on Action 6 will address some of the BEPS concerns related to the issue of dual-resident entities by providing that cases of dual treaty residence would be solved on a case-by-case basis rather than on the basis of the current rule based on place of effective management of entities.

26. This change, however, will not address all BEPS concerns related to dual-resident entities. It will not, for instance, address avoidance strategies resulting from an entity being a resident of a given State under that State's domestic law whilst, at the same time, being a resident of another State under a tax treaty concluded by the first State. The solution to these avoidance strategies must be found in domestic law. Also, the change to Art. 4(3) will not address BEPS concerns that arise from dual-residence where no treaty is involved.

Chapter 9 - Proposed treaty provision on transparent entities

27. The 1999 OECD report on *The Application of the OECD Model Tax Convention to Partnership*[7] (the Partnership Report) contains an extensive analysis of the application of treaty provisions to partnerships, including in situations where there is a mismatch in the tax treatment of the partnership. The Partnership Report, however, did not expressly address the application of tax treaties to entities other than partnerships. In order to address that issue, as well as the fact that some countries have found it difficult to apply the conclusions of the Partnership Report, this Report proposes to include in the OECD Model Tax Convention a new provision and detailed Commentary that will ensure that income of transparent entities is treated, for the purposes of the Convention, in accordance with the principles of the Partnership Report. This will not only ensure that the benefits of tax treaties are granted in appropriate cases but also that these benefits are not granted where neither Contracting State treats, under its domestic law, the income of an entity as the income of one of its residents.

Chapter 10 - Interaction between Part I and tax treaties

28. Chapter 10 of Part II discusses potential treaty issues that could arise from the recommendations in Part I.

29. The first issue is whether treaty issues could arise from the recommended hybrid mismatch rule under which "the payer jurisdiction will deny a deduction for such payment to the extent it gives rise to a D/NI outcome" to neutralise the effect of hybrid mismatches. The Report notes that, apart from the rules of Articles 7 and 24 of the OECD Model Tax Convention, provisions of tax treaties do not govern whether payments are deductible or not and whether they are effectively taxed or not, these being matters of domestic law.

30. The proposed recommendations in Part I also include "defensive" rules under which "[i]f the payer jurisdiction does not neutralise the mismatch then the payee jurisdiction will require such payment to be included in ordinary income to the extent the payment gives rise to a D/NI outcome". The provisions of tax treaties could be implicated if such a rule would seek the imposition of tax on a non-resident whose income would not, under the provisions of the relevant tax treaty, be taxable in that State. The Report concludes, however, that because the definition of "taxpayer" that is applicable for the purposes of the recommendations contemplates the imposition of tax by a jurisdiction only in circumstances where the recipient of the payment is a resident of that jurisdiction or maintains a permanent establishment in that jurisdiction and because the allocative rules of tax treaties generally do not restrict the taxation rights of the State in such

circumstances, treaties should not impact the right of countries to apply the recommendation and any interaction between the recommendation and the provisions of tax treaties should therefore relate primarily to the rules concerning the elimination of double taxation.

31. The Report then proceeds to discuss two recommendations included in Part I that deal with the elimination of double taxation. It first examines the impact of these recommendations with respect to the exemption method and concludes that since it is the credit method, and not the exemption method, that is applicable to dividends under Article 23 A of the OECD Model Tax Convention, no problems should arise from the recommendation that "a dividend exemption that is provided for relief against economic double taxation should not be granted under domestic law to the extent the dividend payment is deductible by the payer".

32. The Report also recognises, however, that a number of bilateral tax treaties provide for the application of the exemption method with respect to dividends received from foreign companies in which a resident company has a substantial shareholding. It notes that problems arising from the inclusion of the exemption method in tax treaties with respect to items of income that are not taxed in the State of source have long been recognised and that because paragraph 4 of Article 23 A may address some situations of hybrid mismatch arrangements where a dividend would otherwise be subject to the exemption method, States that enter into tax treaties providing for the application of the exemption method with respect to dividends should, at a minimum, consider the inclusion of that paragraph in their tax treaties. The Report suggests that a more complete solution would be for States to consider including in their treaties rules that would expressly allow them to apply the credit method, as opposed to the exemption method, with respect to dividends that are deductible in the payer State. These States may also wish to consider a more general solution to the problems of non-taxation resulting from potential abuses of the exemption method, which would be for States not to include the exemption method in their treaties.

33. As regards the application of the credit method, the Report concludes that the recommendation under which relief should be restricted "in proportion to the net taxable income under the arrangement" appears to conform to the domestic tax limitation provided by the credit method described in Article 23 B of the OECD Model Tax Convention. As regards treaties that either supplement, or depart from, the basic approach of Article 23 B, the Report suggests that Contracting States should ensure that their tax treaties provide for the elimination of double taxation without creating opportunities for tax avoidance strategies.

34. The Report finally discusses whether the recommendations in Part I could raise issues with respect to the provisions of Article 24 of the OECD Model Tax Convention concerning non-discrimination. It concludes that, subject to an analysis of the detailed explanations that will be provided in the proposed commentary and the precise wording of the domestic rules that would be drafted to implement the recommendations set out in Part I, these recommendations would not appear to raise concerns about a possible conflict with the provisions of Article 24 of the OECD Model Tax Convention.

Notes

1. See Action 2 – Neutralise the effects of hybrid mismatch arrangements (OECD, 2013a), pp. 15-16.
2. OECD (2010), *Model Tax Convention on Income and on Capital: Condensed Version 2010*, OECD Publishing.
3. See Action 3 – Strengthen CFC rules (OECD, 2013a), pp. 16-17.
4. See Action 4 – Limit base erosion via interest deductions and other financial payments (OECD, 2013a), p. 17.
5. See Action 2 – Neutralise the effects of hybrid mismatch arrangements (OECD, 2013a), pp. 15-16.
6. OECD (2010), *Model Tax Convention on Income and on Capital: Condensed Version 2010*, OECD Publishing.
7. OECD (1999), *The Application of the OECD Model Tax Convention to Partnerships*, Issues in International Taxation, No. 6, OECD Publishing.

Introduction

Previous work undertaken by the OECD on hybrid mismatch arrangements

35. The role played by hybrid mismatch arrangements in aggressive tax planning has been discussed in a number of OECD reports. For example, an OECD report on *Addressing Tax Risks Involving Bank Losses* (OECD, 2010)[1] highlighted their use in the context of international banking and recommended that revenue bodies "bring to the attention of their government tax policy officials those situations which may potentially raise policy issues, and, in particular, those where the same tax loss is relieved in more than one country as a result of differences in tax treatment between jurisdictions, in order to determine whether steps should be taken to eliminate that arbitrage/mismatch opportunity". Similarly the OECD report on *Corporate Loss Utilisation through Aggressive Tax Planning* (OECD, 2011)[2] recommended countries "consider introducing restrictions on the multiple use of the same loss to the extent they are concerned with these results".

36. As a result of concerns raised by a number of OECD member countries, the OECD undertook a review with interested member countries to identify examples of tax planning schemes involving hybrid mismatch arrangements and to assess the effectiveness of response strategies adopted by those countries. That review culminated in a report on *Hybrid Mismatch Arrangements: Tax Policy and Compliance Issues* in 2012 (the Hybrids Report)[3]. The Hybrids Report concludes that the collective tax base of countries is put at risk through the operation of hybrid mismatch arrangements even though it is often difficult to determine unequivocally which individual country has lost tax revenue under the arrangement. Apart from impacting on tax revenues, the Report also concluded that hybrid mismatch arrangements have a negative impact on competition, efficiency, transparency and fairness. The Hybrids Report set out a number of policy options to address such hybrid mismatch arrangements. The Report concluded that domestic law rules which link the tax treatment of an entity, instrument or transfer to the tax treatment in another country had significant

potential as a tool to address hybrid mismatch arrangements. Although such "linking rules" make the application of domestic law more complicated, the Hybrids Report noted that such rules are not a novelty as, in principle, foreign tax credit rules, subject to tax clauses, and controlled foreign company rules often do exactly that.

37. As regards tax treaties, the 1999 OECD report on *The Application of the OECD Model Tax Convention to Partnerships* (the Partnership Report)[4] and the 2010 OECD report on *The Granting of Treaty Benefits with respect to the Income of Collective Investment Vehicles* (the CIV Report)[5] are most directly relevant to Action 2. Both reports contain extensive analysis of the application of treaty provisions to partnerships and CIVs respectively, including in situations where there is a mismatch in the tax treatment of these entities. The main conclusions of the Partnership Report and the CIV report, which have been included in the Commentary of the OECD Model Tax Convention, seek to ensure that the provisions of tax treaties produce appropriate results when applied to partnerships and CIVs, in particular in the case of a partnership or CIV that constitutes a hybrid entity. These reports, however, did not expressly address the application of tax treaties to entities other than partnerships and CIVs.

BEPS Action Plan

38. The OECD Committee of Fiscal Affairs (CFA) approved the BEPS Action Plan at their meeting on 25 June 2013. The Action Plan was subsequently endorsed by G-20 Finance Ministers at their meeting in Moscow on 19-20 July 2013[6] and in the meeting of the G-20 Heads of Government in Saint Petersburg, on 5-6 September 2013[7].

39. Action 2 calls for the development of "model treaty provisions and recommendations regarding the design of domestic rules to neutralise the effect of hybrid instruments and entities." The Action item states that "this may include:

(i) changes to the OECD Model Tax Convention to ensure that hybrid instruments and entities (as well as dual resident entities) are not used to obtain the benefits of treaties unduly;

(ii) domestic law provisions that prevent exemption or non-recognition for payments that are deductible by the payor;

(iii) domestic law provisions that deny a deduction for a payment that is not includible in income by the recipient (and is not subject to taxation under controlled foreign company (CFC) or similar rules);

(iv) domestic law provisions that deny a deduction for a payment that is also deductible in another jurisdiction; and

(v) where necessary, guidance on co-ordination or tie-breaker rules if more than one country seeks to apply such rules to a transaction or structure."

40. This Report sets out the recommendations for the design of domestic law and model treaty provisions that are called for under Action 2. Part I sets out the domestic law recommendations and Part II sets out recommended changes to the OECD Model Tax Convention to ensure that hybrid instruments are not used to obtain undue treaty benefits.

Notes

1. OECD (2010), *Addressing Tax Risks Involving Bank Losses*, OECD Publishing.

2. OECD (2011), *Corporate Loss Utilisation through Aggressive Tax Planning*, OECD, Paris.

3. OECD (2012), *Hybrid Mismatch Arrangements: Tax Policy and Compliance Issues,* OECD, Paris.

4. OECD (1999), *The Application of the OECD Model Tax Convention to Partnerships*, Issues in International Taxation, No. 6, OECD Publishing.

5. OECD (2012), "R(24). The granting of treaty benefits with respect to the income of collective investment vehicles", in OECD, *Model Tax Convention on Income and on Capital 2010 (Full Version)*, OECD Publishing.

6. "*Closing tax gaps - OECD launches Action Plan on Base Erosion and Profit Shifting*", news release on 19/07/2013, www.oecd.org/newsroom/closing-tax-gaps-oecd-launches-action-plan-on-base-erosion-and-profit-shifting.htm.

7. See Secretary-General Report to the G20 leaders, St Petersbourg, Russia, 5-6 September 2013, www.oecd.org/tax/SG-report-G20-Leaders-StPetersburg.pdf.

Bibliography

OECD (2012), "R(24). The granting of treaty benefits with respect to the income of collective investment vehicles", in OECD, *Model Tax Convention on Income and on Capital 2010 (Full Version)*, OECD Publishing.
http://dx.doi.org/10.1787/9789264175181-117-en

OECD (2012), *Hybrid Mismatch Arrangements: Tax Policy and Compliance Issues,* OECD, Paris.
www.oecd.org/ctp/aggressive/hybridmismatcharrangementstaxpolicyandcomplianceissues.htm

OECD (2011), *Corporate Loss Utilisation through Aggressive Tax Planning*, OECD Publishing.
http://dx.doi.org/10.1787/9789264119222-en

OECD (2010), *Model Tax Convention on Income and on Capital: Condensed Version 2010*, OECD Publishing.
http://dx.doi.org/10.1787/mtc_cond-2010-en

OECD (2010), *Addressing Tax Risks Involving Bank Losses*, OECD Publishing.
http://dx.doi.org/10.1787/9789264088689-en

OECD (1999),*The Application of the OECD Model Tax Convention to Partnerships*, Issues in International Taxation, No. 6, OECD Publishing.
http://dx.doi.org/10.1787/9789264173316-en

Part I

Recommendations for the design of domestic rules

Chapter 1

Definition of hybrid mismatch arrangement

41. A hybrid mismatch arrangement is an arrangement that exploits a difference in the tax treatment of an entity or instrument under the laws of two or more tax jurisdictions to produce a mismatch in tax outcomes where that mismatch has the effect of lowering the aggregate tax burden of the parties to the arrangement.

Arrangement results in a mismatch in the tax treatment of a payment

42. The focus of Action 2 is on arrangements that exploit differences in the way cross-border payments are treated for tax purposes in the jurisdiction of the payer and payee and only to the extent such difference in treatment results in a mismatch.

43. The extent of a mismatch is determined by comparing the tax treatment of the payment under the laws of each jurisdiction where the mismatch arises. A D/NI mismatch generally occurs when the proportion of a payment that is deductible under the laws of one jurisdiction does not correspond to the proportion that is included in ordinary income by any other jurisdiction. A DD mismatch arises to the extent that all or part of the payment is deductible under the laws of another jurisdiction.

44. All the mismatch arrangements described above involve payments. The amount of a payment is measured in money. While differences in the way two jurisdictions value a payment can give rise to mismatches, differences in the valuation of money itself are not within the scope of the hybrid mismatch rule. For example, gains and losses from foreign currency fluctuations on a loan are differences in the value of money (rather than the amount of money) payable under that loan. This kind of mismatch will not give rise to a D/NI outcome provided the proportion of the interest and principal payable under the loan is the same under the laws of both jurisdictions.

45. The hybrid mismatch rules do not extend to payments that are only deemed to be made for tax purposes and that do not involve the creation of economic rights between the parties. Rules, for example, that entitle taxpayers to a unilateral tax deduction for invested equity without requiring the taxpayer to accrue any expenditure (such as regimes that grant "deemed" interest deductions for equity capital) are economically closer to a tax exemption or similar taxpayer specific concessions and do not produce a mismatch in tax outcomes in the sense contemplated by Action Item 2. Such rules and rules having similar effect should, however, be considered further, either separately or in the context of Action Item 4 on Interest Deductibility.

Arrangement contains a hybrid element that causes a mismatch in tax outcomes

46. While cross-border mismatches arise in other contexts (such as the payment of deductible interest to a tax exempt entity) the only types of mismatches targeted by this Report are those that rely on a hybrid element to produce D/NI and DD outcomes.

47. As identified in Action 2, hybrid mismatch arrangements can be divided into two distinct categories based on their underlying mechanics: some arrangements involve the use of hybrid entities, where the same entity is treated differently under the laws of two or more jurisdictions; and others involve the use of hybrid instruments, where there is a conflict in the treatment of the same instrument under the laws of two or more jurisdictions. In both cases the hybrid element leads to a different characterisation of a payment under the laws of different jurisdictions.

48. Conflicts in the treatment of the hybrid entity generally involve a conflict between the transparency or opacity of the entity for tax purposes in relation to a particular payment. Within the category of hybrid instruments there is a further subdivision that can be made between hybrid transfers, which are arrangements in relation to an asset where taxpayers in two jurisdictions take mutually incompatible positions in relation to the character of the ownership rights in that asset, and hybrid financial instruments, which are financial instruments that result in taxpayers taking mutually incompatible positions in relation to the treatment of the same payment made under the instrument.

49. In most cases the causal connection between the hybrid element and the mismatch will be obvious. There are some challenges, however, in identifying the hybrid element in the context of hybrid financial instruments. Because of the wide variety of financial instruments and the different ways jurisdictions tax them, it has proven impossible, in practice, for this Report

to comprehensively identify and accurately define all those situations where cross-border conflicts in the characterisation of a payment under a financing instrument may lead to a mismatch in tax treatment. Rather than targeting these technical differences, the focus of this Report is on aligning the treatment of cross-border payments under a financial instrument so that amounts that are treated as a financing expense by the issuer's jurisdiction are treated as ordinary income in the holder's jurisdiction. Accordingly this Report recommends that a financial instrument should be treated as hybrid where the terms of the instrument would have been sufficient to bring about such a mismatch in tax outcomes.

Mismatch in tax outcomes lowers the aggregate tax paid by the parties to the arrangement

50. The hybrid mismatch rules should not generally interfere with hybrid entities or instruments that produce outcomes that do not raise tax policy concerns. In order to fall within the scope of the rule, the arrangement should result in an erosion of the tax base of one or more jurisdictions where the arrangement is structured. For example, the hybrid mismatch rule limiting D/NI outcomes should not generally address differences in the timing of payments and receipts under the laws of different jurisdictions and the rules limiting DD outcomes for hybrid entity payments should generally preserve both deductions to the extent they are offset against income that is taxable under the laws of both jurisdictions or to the extent the DD outcome simply results in shifting the net income of the taxpayer from one taxable period to another.

Chapter 2

Arrangements that produce D/NI outcomes

Recommended hybrid mismatch rule for financial instruments

51. This section sets out recommendations for the design of hybrid mismatch rules to neutralise the effect of hybrid financial instruments. The hybrid financial instrument rule applies to any financial instrument that is subject to a different tax treatment under the law of two or more jurisdictions such that a payment under that instrument gives rise to a mismatch in tax outcomes. A hybrid financial instrument includes a hybrid transfer.

Hybrid financial instruments

52. A simplified illustration of a mismatch arrangement involving the use of a hybrid financial instrument is set out in Figure 2.1.

Figure 2.1 Hybrid Financial Instrument

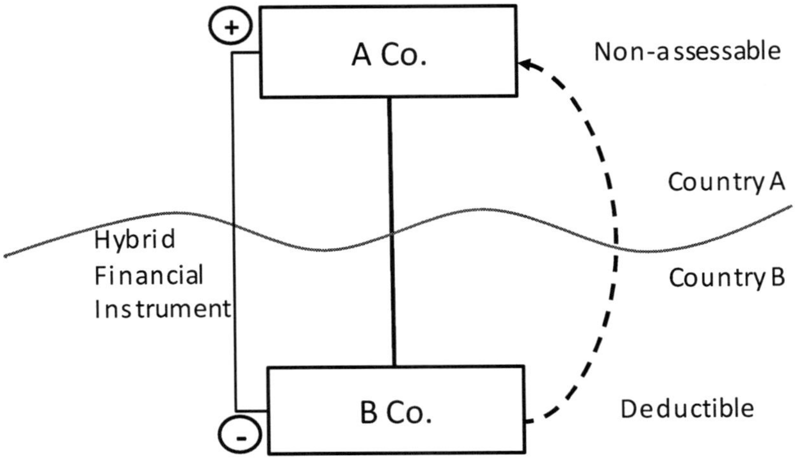

53. In this example B Co (an entity resident in Country B) issues a hybrid financial instrument to A Co (an entity resident in Country A). The instrument is treated as debt for the purposes of Country B law and Country B grants a deduction for interest payments made under the instrument while Country A law does not tax the payment or grants some form of tax relief (an exemption, exclusion, indirect tax credit, etc.) in relation to the interest payments received under that instrument.

54. This mismatch can be due to a number of reasons. Most commonly the financial instrument is treated by the issuer as *debt* and by the holder as *equity*. This difference in characterisation often results in a payment of deductible interest by the issuer being treated as a dividend which is exempted from the charge to tax in the holder's jurisdiction or subject to some other form of equivalent tax relief. In other cases the mismatch in tax outcomes may not be attributable to a general difference in the characterisation of an instrument for tax purposes but rather to a specific difference in the tax treatment of a particular payment made under the instrument. For example the hybrid financial instrument might be an optional convertible note where B Co is entitled to a deduction for the value of the embedded option while A Co ignores the value of the option component or gives it a lower value than the B Co. This difference in tax treatment may result in a portion of the payment under the instrument being deductible under the laws of Country B but not included in ordinary income under the laws of Country A.

Hybrid transfers

55. Hybrid transfers are typically a particular type of collateralised loan arrangement or derivative transaction where the counterparties to the same arrangement in different jurisdictions both treat themselves as the owner of the loan collateral or subject matter of the derivative. This difference in the way the arrangement is characterised can lead to payments made under the instrument producing a mismatch in tax outcomes.

56. While the legal mechanisms for achieving a hybrid transfer depend on the individual tax rules of the jurisdictions involved, the most common transaction used to achieve a mismatch in tax outcomes under a hybrid transfer is a sale and repurchase arrangement (generally referred to as a "repo") over an asset where the terms of the repo make it the economic equivalent to a collateralised loan. A repo can give rise to a mismatch in tax outcomes where one jurisdiction treats the arrangement in accordance with its form (a sale and a repurchase of the asset) while the counterparty jurisdiction taxes the arrangement in accordance with its economic substance (a loan with the asset serving as collateral). While the collateral for these arrangements often involves shares of controlled entities, the same repo technique can be used with virtually any asset that generates an

excluded or exempt return or some other tax relief under the laws of both jurisdictions.

57. A basic example of such a structure is illustrated in Figure 2.2.

Figure 2.2 Collateralised Loan Repo

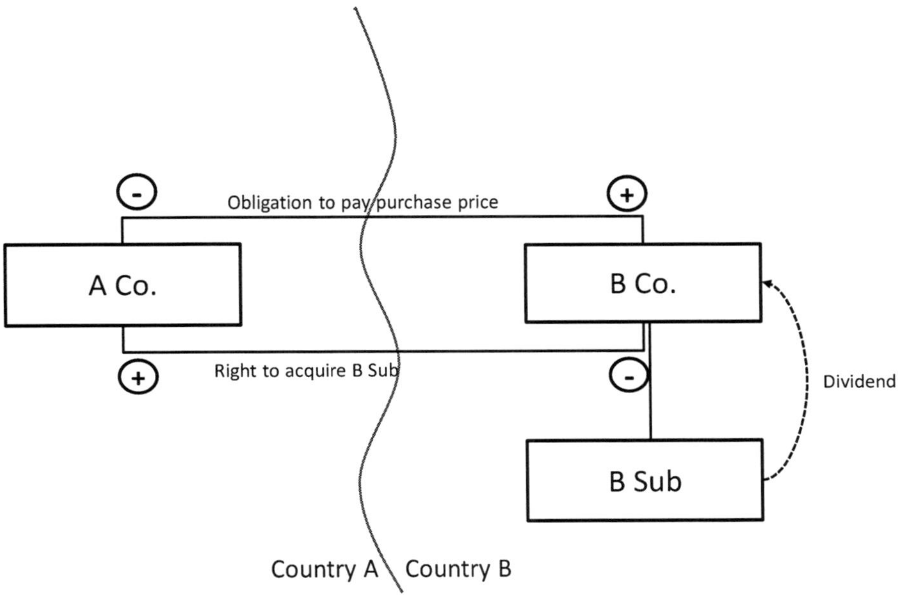

58. The structure illustrated in Figure 2.2 involves a company in Country A (A Co) which owns a subsidiary (B Sub). A sells the shares of B Sub to B Co under an arrangement that A Co (or an affiliate) will acquire those shares at a future date for an agreed price. Between sale and repurchase, B Sub makes distributions on the shares to B Co.

59. The net cost of the repo to A Co is treated as a deductible financing cost. A Co's cost includes the B Sub dividends that are paid to and retained by B Co. Country B will typically grant a credit, exclusion, exemption or some other tax relief to B Co on the dividends received. B Co also treats the transfer of the shares back to A Co as a genuine sale of shares and may exempt any gain on disposal under an equity participation exemption or a general exclusion for capital gains. The combined effect of the repo transaction is, therefore, to generate a deduction for A Co in respect of the aggregate payments made under the repo with no corresponding inclusion for B Co.

Recommended rule

60. The response recommended in this Report is to neutralise the effect of hybrid mismatches that arise under financial instruments (including hybrid transfers) through the adoption of a linking rule that aligns the tax outcomes for the payer and payee under a financial instrument. This Report recommends that the primary response should be to deny the payer a deduction for payments made under a hybrid financial instrument, with the payee jurisdiction applying a defensive rule that would require a deductible payment to be included in ordinary income in the event the payer was located in a jurisdiction that did not apply a hybrid mismatch rule to eliminate the mismatch.

61. In general, reasonable differences in timing of the recognition of payments do not constitute a mismatch in tax outcomes. Further detail will be agreed in the Commentary on the circumstances and requirements for establishing permissible differences in the timing of recognition of payments under the hybrid financing instrument rule.

62. Because of the wide variety of financial instruments and the different ways jurisdictions tax them, it has proven impossible, in practice, for this Report to comprehensively identify and accurately define all those situations where cross-border conflicts in the characterisation of a payment under a financial instrument may lead to a mismatch in tax treatment. Rather than targeting these technical differences the focus of this Report is on aligning the treatment of cross-border payments under a financial instrument so that amounts that are treated as a financing expense by the issuer's jurisdiction are treated as ordinary income in the holder's jurisdiction. Accordingly the rule recommended in this section provides that a financial instrument should be treated as a hybrid financial instrument where the terms of the instrument would have been sufficient to bring about a mismatch in tax outcomes.

63. The rule only applies to a financial instrument held by a related party or as part of a structured arrangement and does not apply in certain defined circumstances.

64. Public submissions raise concerns as to the potential impact of the hybrid financial instrument rule on a financial instrument entered into by a taxpayer on-market where that taxpayer regularly enters into similar financial instruments on the same terms with unrelated parties as part of its ordinary trading activities. Public submissions suggest that the application of the hybrid financial instrument rule to the taxpayer may, in some circumstances, place a disproportionate and undue compliance burden on such markets. We will be looking to financial institutions to provide further input that will allow for a better understanding of the case for excluding or

better targeting the application of the hybrid financial instrument rule in these circumstances.

65. Recommended language for a domestic law hybrid mismatch rule is set out in the box below:

Recommendation 1.
Hybrid financial instrument rule

The following rule should apply to a payment under a financial instrument that results in a hybrid mismatch (as defined in paragraph 3 below).

1 Neutralise the mismatch to the extent payment gives rise to a D/NI Outcome

(a) Response – deny the deduction

The payer jurisdiction will deny a deduction for such payment to the extent it gives rise to a D/NI outcome.

(b) Defensive rule – require the payment to be included in ordinary income

If the payer jurisdiction does not neutralise the mismatch then the payee jurisdiction will require such payment to be included in ordinary income to the extent the payment gives rise to a D/NI outcome.

(c) Timing differences

Differences in the timing of the recognition of payments will not be treated as giving rise to a D/NI outcome for a payment made under a financial instrument, provided the taxpayer can establish to the satisfaction of a tax authority that the payment will be included as ordinary income within a reasonable period of time. Further guidance will be provided in the Commentary on the circumstances and requirements for such proof.

2 Rule only applies to payments under a financial instrument (including a hybrid transfer)

(a) Financial instrument

A financial instrument includes any arrangement that is taxed under the rules for taxing debt, equity or derivatives under the laws of the payee and payer jurisdictions and includes any hybrid transfer.

Recommendation 1. *(Cont.)*

Any arrangement where one person provides money to another in consideration for a financing or equity return shall also be treated as a financial instrument to the extent of such financing or equity return.

(b) *Hybrid transfer*

A hybrid transfer is any asset transfer arrangement entered into by a taxpayer with another party where:

- the taxpayer is the owner of the asset and the rights of the counterparty in respect of that asset are treated as obligations of the taxpayer; and
- under the laws of the counterparty jurisdiction, the counterparty is the owner of the asset and the rights of the taxpayer in respect of that asset are treated as obligations of the counterparty.

Ownership of an asset for these purposes includes any rules that result in the taxpayer being taxed as the beneficial owner of the corresponding cash-flows from the asset.

3 Rule only applies to payments that result in a hybrid mismatch

(a) A payment results in a hybrid mismatch where the terms of the instrument result in a mismatch in the tax treatment of payments made under the financial instrument.

(b) The terms of the instrument result in a mismatch in the tax treatment of payments made under the financial instrument if the mismatch would have arisen had the same instrument been directly entered into between resident taxpayers of ordinary status under the laws of their respective jurisdictions.

4 Scope of the Rule

(a) This rule only applies to a financial instrument entered into with a related person or where the payment is made under a structured arrangement and the taxpayer is party to that structured arrangement.

5 Exceptions to the Rule

(a) *Regimes where the tax policy of the deduction under the laws of the payer jurisdiction is to preserve tax neutrality for the payer and payee*

Recommendation 1. *(Cont.)*

The primary response in paragraph 1(a) should not apply to a payment by an investment vehicle that is subject to special regulation and tax treatment under the laws of the establishment jurisdiction in circumstances where:

(i) the tax policy of the establishment jurisdiction is to preserve the deduction for the payment under the financial instrument to ensure that:

- the taxpayer is subject to no or minimal taxation on its investment income; and
- that holders of financial instruments issued by the taxpayer are subject to tax on that payment as ordinary income on a current basis.

(ii) the regulatory and tax framework in the establishment jurisdiction has the effect that the financial instruments issued by the investment vehicle will result in all or substantially all of the taxpayer's investment income being paid and distributed to the holders of those financial instruments within a reasonable period of time after that income was derived or received by the taxpayer;

(iii) the tax policy of the establishment jurisdiction is that the full amount of the payment is:

- included in the ordinary income of any person that is a payee in the establishment jurisdiction; and
- not excluded from the ordinary income of any person that is a payee under the laws of the payee jurisdiction under a treaty between the establishment jurisdiction and the payee jurisdiction; and

(iv) the payment is not made under a structured arrangement.

Further guidance will be provided in the Commentary on the circumstances where the exception will apply and the requirements for the application of this exception. The defensive rule in 1(b) will continue to apply to any payment made by such an investment vehicle.

Other recommendations for the tax treatment of financial instruments

66. This section sets out recommendations for changes to domestic law that would better align tax outcomes on cross-border transactions with their intended policy and reduce the mismatches arising through the use of hybrid financial instruments.

Denial of dividend exemption for deductible payments

67. The first recommendation targets mismatches that arise in respect of the structures identified in Figure 2.1. As noted above, mismatches can arise in respect of payments made under a financial instrument that is a debt / equity hybrid. This difference in characterisation often results in a payment of deductible interest by the issuer being treated as a dividend which is exempted from the charge to tax in the holder's jurisdiction or subject to some other form of equivalent tax relief.

68. A country that provides for a dividend exemption specifically to relieve economic double taxation on distributed profit should restrict such exemption to payments that are paid out of after-tax profits. In a wholly-domestic situation this outcome can generally be achieved by restricting the dividend exemption to payments that are characterised as dividends or distributions under domestic law. In cross-border payment situations, however, such a restriction will not be sufficient, as the domestic criteria characterising the payment and determining its tax treatment will not apply to the payer. Jurisdictions that relieve economic double taxation by offering a dividend exemption for amounts paid by a foreign payer should therefore similarly limit the benefit of the dividend exemption to payments that are paid out of after-tax profits.

69. The payee jurisdiction should not be required to extend relief from economic double taxation under domestic law in circumstances where the payment has not borne underlying tax. The Report therefore recommends that jurisdictions which offer an exemption for dividends do not extend that exemption to deductible payments. This recommendation is not subject to the same limitations as to scope that apply to the hybrid financial instrument rule. Jurisdictions should also give further consideration to whether a recommendation in respect of the dividend exemption should apply to other types of double tax relief granted for dividends.

Limitation of credits for taxes withheld at source

70. The second specific recommendation targets mismatches in the crediting of withholding taxes that arise in respect of the structures identified in Figure 2.2. In order to prevent taxpayers in a repo transaction

claiming two tax credits in respect of the same source taxation, this Report recommends that a taxpayer's entitlement to direct tax credits under a hybrid transfer be restricted in proportion to the taxpayer's net income under the arrangement.

71. Recommended language for the tax treatment of financial instruments is set out in the box below:

Recommendation 2.
Specific recommendations for the tax treatment of financial instruments

1 Denial of dividend exemption for deductible payments

In order to prevent D/NI outcomes from arising under a financial instrument, a dividend exemption that is provided for relief against economic double taxation should not be granted under domestic law to the extent the dividend payment is deductible by the payer. Equally, jurisdictions should consider adopting similar restrictions for other types of dividend relief granted to relieve economic double taxation on underlying profits.

2 Limitation of tax credits for tax withheld at source

In order to prevent duplication of tax credits under a hybrid transfer, any jurisdiction that grants relief for tax withheld at source on a payment made under a hybrid transfer should restrict the benefit of such relief in proportion to the net taxable income of the taxpayer under the arrangement.

3 Scope

There is no limitation as to the scope of these recommendations.

Recommended hybrid mismatch rule for disregarded payments made by a hybrid payer

72. This section sets out recommendations for the design of hybrid mismatch rules to prevent a hybrid payer making a deductible payment under the laws of the payer jurisdiction that is disregarded under the laws of the payee jurisdiction. The hybrid mismatch rule applies where the tax treatment of the payer under the laws of the payee jurisdiction causes a deductible payment to be disregarded under the laws of the payee jurisdiction. A simple example of such a structure is illustrated in Figure 2.3.

Figure 2.3 Disregarded Payments Made by a Hybrid Entity to a Related Party

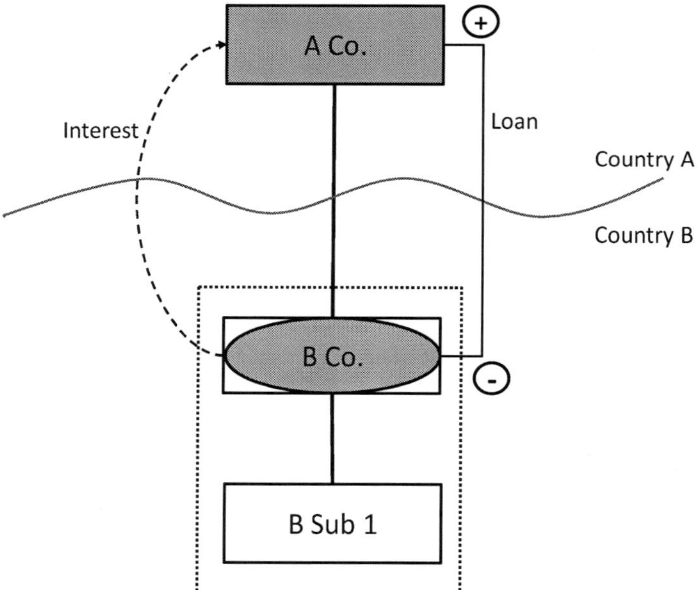

73. In this example, A Co holds all the shares of a foreign subsidiary (B Co). B Co is a hybrid entity that is disregarded for Country A tax purposes. B Co borrows from A Co and pays interest on the loan. B Co is treated as transparent under the laws of Country A and (because A Co is the only shareholder in B Co) Country A simply disregards the separate existence of B Co. Disregarding B Co means that the loan (and by extension the interest on the loan) between A Co and B Co is ignored under the laws of Country A.

74. B Co is consolidated, for tax purposes, with its operating subsidiary B Sub 1 which allows it to surrender the tax benefit of the interest deduction to B Sub 1. The ability to "surrender" the tax benefit through the

consolidation regime allows the deduction for the interest expense to be set-off against income that will not be taxable under the laws of Country A.

Recommended rule

75. The response recommended in this Report is to neutralise the effect of hybrid mismatches that arise under disregarded hybrid payments through the adoption of a linking rule that aligns the tax outcomes for the payer and payee. This Report recommends that the primary response should be to deny the payer a deduction for payments made under a disregarded payment with the payee jurisdiction applying a defensive rule that would require a disregarded payment to be included in ordinary income in the event the payer was located in a jurisdiction that did not apply a hybrid mismatch rule.

76. The hybrid mismatch rule does not apply, however, to the extent the deduction for the disregarded payment is set off against "dual inclusion income", which is income that is taken into account as ordinary income under the laws of both the payer and payee jurisdiction.

77. In order to address timing differences in the recognition of deductions for disregarded payments and dual inclusion income any excess deduction (i.e. net loss) from such disregarded payments that cannot be set off against dual inclusion income in the current period remains eligible to be set-off against dual inclusion income that arises in another period under the ordinary rules that allow for the carry-forward (or back) of losses to other taxable periods.

78. This rule only applies if the parties to the mismatch are in the same control group or where the payment is made under a structured arrangement and the taxpayer is party to that structured arrangement.

79. Recommended language for a domestic law hybrid mismatch rule is set out in the box below:

Recommendation 3.
Disregarded hybrid payments rule

The following rule should apply to a disregarded payment made by a hybrid payer that results in a hybrid mismatch (as defined in paragraph 3 below).

1 Neutralise the mismatch to the extent payment gives rise to D/NI Outcome

(a) Response – deny the deduction

The payer jurisdiction will deny a deduction for such payment to the extent it gives rise to a D/NI outcome.

(b) Defensive rule – require the payment to be included in ordinary income

If the payer jurisdiction does not neutralise the mismatch then the payee jurisdiction will require such payment to be included in ordinary income to the extent the payment gives rise to a D/NI outcome.

(c) Mismatch does not arise to the extent the deduction is set off against dual inclusion income

No mismatch will arise to the extent that the deduction in the payer jurisdiction is set-off against income that is included in ordinary income under the laws of both the payee and the payer jurisdiction (i.e. dual inclusion income).

(d) Treatment of excess deduction

Any deduction that exceeds the amount of dual inclusion income (the excess deduction) may be eligible to be set-off against dual inclusion income in another period.

2 Rule only applies to disregarded payments made by a hybrid payer

(a) A disregarded payment is payment that is deductible under the laws of the payer jurisdiction and is not recognised under the laws of the payee jurisdiction.

(b) A person will be a hybrid payer where the tax treatment of the payer under the laws of the payee jurisdiction causes the payment to be a disregarded payment.

Recommendation 3. *(Cont.)*

3 Rule only applies to hybrid mismatches

A disregarded payment made by a hybrid payer results in a hybrid mismatch if, under the laws of the payer jurisdiction, the deduction may be set-off against income that is not dual inclusion income.

4 Scope of the Rule

This rule only applies if the parties to the mismatch are in the same control group or where the payment is made under a structured arrangement and the taxpayer is party to that structured arrangement.

Recommended hybrid mismatch rule for reverse hybrids

80. D/NI tax outcomes can also arise out of payments made to a hybrid payee. The hybrid in this case is usually described as a reverse hybrid because, in a reversal of the examples considered above the hybrid is treated as opaque by its foreign investor and transparent under the jurisdiction where it is established. Figure 2.4 illustrates a basic structure using a reverse hybrid technique.

Figure 2.4 Payment to a Foreign Reverse Hybrid

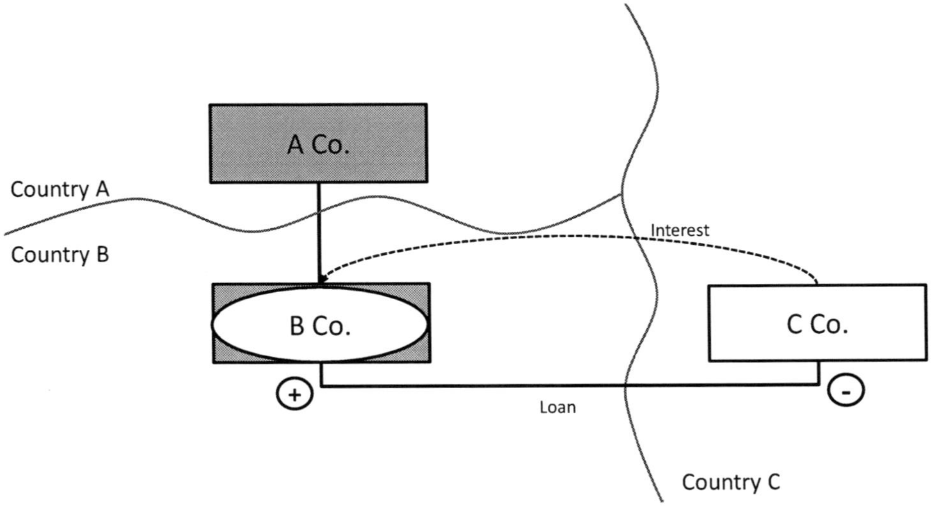

81. In this structure A Co, a company resident in Country A (the investor jurisdiction) owns all of the shares in B Co, a foreign subsidiary established under the laws of Country B (the establishment jurisdiction). B Co is treated as transparent for tax purposes under the laws of Country B but is regarded as a separate taxable entity under the laws of Country A. C Co, a company resident in Country C (the payer jurisdiction) borrows money from B Co and makes interest payments under the loan.

82. Payments made to a reverse hybrid can give rise to D/NI outcomes if the payment is deductible under the laws of the payer jurisdiction (Country C) but is not included in income under the laws of either the investor or the establishment jurisdiction (Country A or B) because neither the investor nor the establishment jurisdiction treats the payment as income of a resident (or, more specifically, each country treats the income as being derived by a resident of the other jurisdiction).

Recommended rule

83. The response recommended in this Report is to neutralise the effect of hybrid mismatches that arise under payments made to reverse hybrids through the adoption of a linking rule that denies a deduction for such payments to the extent they give rise to a D/NI outcome. This Report only recommends the adoption of the primary response of denying the payer a deduction for payments made to a reverse hybrid. A defensive rule is unnecessary given Recommendation 5.

84. Payments to a reverse hybrid will not generally give rise to timing differences in the recognition of payments.

85. This rule only applies if the parties to the mismatch (A Co, B Co and C Co in the above example) are in the same control group or where the payment is made under a structured arrangement and the taxpayer is party to that structured arrangement.

86. Recommended language for a domestic law hybrid mismatch rule is set out in the box below:

Recommendation 4.
Reverse hybrid rule

The following rule should apply to a payment made to a reverse hybrid that results in a hybrid mismatch (as defined in paragraph 3 below).

1 Neutralise the mismatch to extent payment gives rise to D/NI Outcome

(a) Response - Deny the Deduction

The payer jurisdiction will deny a deduction for such payment to the extent it gives rise to a D/NI outcome.

2 Rule only applies to payments made to a reverse hybrid

A reverse hybrid is any person that is treated as a separate entity by a related investor and as transparent under the laws of the establishment jurisdiction.

3 Rule only applies to hybrid mismatches

A payment results in a hybrid mismatch if a mismatch would not have arisen had the accrued income been paid directly to the investor.

4 Scope

The rule only applies to any payer that is in the same control group as the parties to the hybrid mismatch or if the payment is part of a structured arrangement and the payer is party to that arrangement.

Specific recommendations for the tax treatment of reverse hybrids

Application of CFC or other offshore investment regimes

87. In the context of reverse hybrids the risk of any mismatch can be eliminated by the investor jurisdiction applying an offshore investment regime (such as a CFC regime) that taxes income accrued through offshore investment structures on a current basis. A number of jurisdictions already have offshore investment regimes that could apply to the accrued income of reverse hybrids.

88. In certain circumstances, however, offshore investment regimes are not fully effective to tax, on a current basis, income of residents accrued through reverse hybrids. In these cases jurisdictions should introduce specific rules to bring the income of a reverse hybrid within the charge to taxation in the investor jurisdiction. As discussed in Chapter 4 similar D/NI outcomes can arise under

imported mismatch arrangements and CFC or other offshore investment regimes may be effective to address such mismatches. In order to address the risk of such mismatches, this Report therefore recommends that jurisdictions introduce, or make changes to, their offshore investment regimes in order to prevent D/NI outcomes from arising in respect of payments to a reverse hybrid. Equally jurisdictions should consider introducing or making changes to their offshore investment regimes in relation to imported mismatches. Tax policy responses could include measures such as treating the intermediary as resident in the investor jurisdiction, treating the intermediary as transparent or taxing the resident holder on a deemed distribution or changes in market value of the investment in the offshore investment structure. These measures may be further considered as part of the work on Action 3.[1]

Limiting tax transparency for reverse hybrids controlled by non-resident investors

89. No D/NI outcome will arise in respect of a reverse hybrid if the intermediary jurisdiction exerts taxing jurisdiction over the reverse hybrid either by treating all the income as sourced in the intermediary jurisdiction (due to the intermediary maintaining a permanent establishment or some other form of taxable presence in that jurisdiction) or due to the intermediary jurisdiction treating the reverse hybrid as resident in that jurisdiction in certain defined circumstances.

90. This Report recommends that jurisdictions adopt a rule that would re-characterise transparent entities established in the intermediary jurisdiction as tax resident in circumstances where a non-resident controlling investor's share of the reverse hybrid's net income is not within the charge to taxation under the laws of the establishment jurisdiction or the investor jurisdiction.

Information reporting for intermediaries

91. It can be difficult for both investors and tax administrations to obtain sufficient information on what income has been accumulated in the offshore fund and how much has been allocated to a resident investor. For this reason the Report recommends the development of guidance for tax filing and information reporting requirements that would facilitate the ability of non-resident investors and tax administrations to determine the income and gains derived by the entity and amounts allocated to each investor.

92. Recommended language for the tax treatment of reverse hybrids is set out in the box below:

Recommendation 5.
Specific recommendations for the tax treatment of reverse hybrids and imported mismatches

1 Improvements to CFC or other offshore investment regimes

Jurisdictions should introduce, or make changes to, their offshore investment regimes in order to prevent D/NI outcomes from arising in respect of payments to a reverse hybrid. Equally jurisdictions should consider introducing or making changes to their offshore investment regimes in relation to imported mismatch arrangements.

2 Limiting tax transparency for non-resident investors

A reverse hybrid should be treated as a resident taxpayer in the establishment jurisdiction if the income of the reverse hybrid is not brought within the charge to taxation under the laws of the establishment jurisdiction and the accrued income of a non-resident investor in the same control group as the reverse hybrid is not brought within the charge to taxation under the laws of the investor jurisdiction.

3 Information reporting for intermediaries

Further detail will be provided in the Commentary on the circumstances where the establishment jurisdiction should impose appropriate tax filing or information reporting requirements on the reverse hybrid to facilitate the ability of non-resident investors and tax administrations to determine the income and gains derived by the reverse hybrid and the accrued income of non-resident investors. This will need to take account of other work for instance on the CRS and TRACE as well as the interaction with Action 12 of the BEPS Action Plan.

Note

1 See Action 3 – Strengthen CFC rules (OECD, 2013), pp. 16-17.

Bibliography

OECD (2013), *Action Plan on Base Erosion and Profit Shifting*, OECD Publishing.
http://dx.doi.org/10.1787/9789264202719-en.

Chapter 3

Arrangements that produce DD outcomes

Recommended hybrid mismatch rule for deductible payments made by a hybrid payer

93. This section sets out recommendations for the design of hybrid mismatch rules to prevent a deductible payment made by a hybrid payer triggering a duplicate deduction under the laws of the parent jurisdiction. The most common DD hybrid technique involves the use of a hybrid subsidiary that is treated as transparent under the laws of the investor's tax jurisdiction and opaque under the laws of the jurisdiction where it is established or operates. This hybrid treatment can result in the same item of expenditure incurred by the hybrid being deductible under the laws of both the parent and payer jurisdictions. Figure 3.1 illustrates a simple arrangement utilising this technique.

Figure 3.1 Basic Double Deduction Structure Using Hybrid Entity

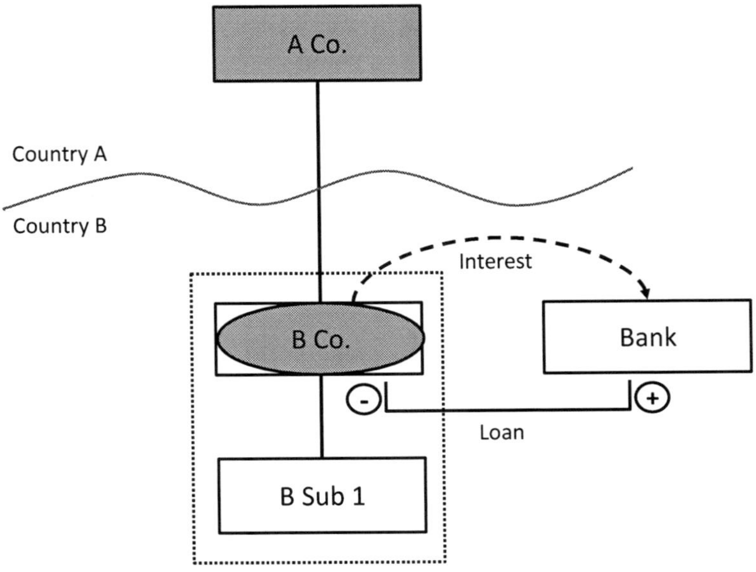

94. In this example, A Co holds all the shares of a foreign subsidiary (B Co). B Co is disregarded for Country A tax purposes. B Co borrows from a bank and pays interest on the loan. B Co derives no other income. Because B Co is disregarded, A Co is treated as the borrower under the loan for the purposes of Country A's tax laws. The arrangement therefore gives rise to an interest deduction under the laws of both Country B and Country A.

95. B Co is consolidated, for tax purposes, with its operating subsidiary B Sub 1 which allows it to surrender the tax benefit of the interest deduction to B Sub 1. The ability to "surrender" the tax benefit through the consolidation regime allows the two deductions for the interest expense to be set-off against separate income arising in Country A and Country B.

96. The creation of a permanent establishment in the payer jurisdiction, that is eligible to consolidate with other taxpayers in the same jurisdiction, can be used to achieve similar DD outcomes.

Recommended rule

97. The response recommended in this Report is to neutralise the effect of hybrid mismatches that arise under such DD structures through the adoption of a linking rule that aligns the tax outcomes in the payer and parent jurisdictions. The hybrid mismatch rule isolates the hybrid element in the structure by identifying a deductible payment made by a hybrid payer in the payer jurisdiction and the corresponding "duplicate deduction" generated in the parent jurisdiction. The primary response is that the duplicate deduction cannot be claimed in the parent jurisdiction to the extent it exceeds the claimant's dual inclusion income (income brought into account for tax purposes under the laws of both jurisdictions). A defensive rule applies in the payer jurisdiction to prevent the hybrid payer claiming the benefit of a deductible payment against non-dual inclusion income if the primary rule does not apply.

98. In the case of both the primary and defensive rules, the excess deductions can be offset against dual inclusion income in another period. In order to prevent stranded losses, it is recommended that excess duplicate deductions should be allowed to the extent that the taxpayer can establish, to the satisfaction of the tax administration, that the deduction cannot be set-off against the income of any person under the laws of the other jurisdiction.

99. There is no limitation on the scope of the primary response however the defensive rule only applies if the parties to the mismatch are in the same control group or where the payment is made under a structured arrangement and the taxpayer is party to that structured arrangement. Recommended language for a domestic law hybrid mismatch rule is set out in the box below:

Recommendation 6.
Deductible hybrid payments rule

The following rule should apply to a hybrid payer that makes a payment that is deductible under the laws of the payer jurisdiction and that triggers a duplicate deduction in the parent jurisdiction that results in a hybrid mismatch (as defined in paragraph 3 below).

1 Neutralise the mismatch to the extent payment gives rise to DD Outcome

(a) Response - Deny the deduction in the parent jurisdiction

The parent jurisdiction will deny the duplicate deduction for such payment to the extent it gives rise to a DD outcome.

(b) Defensive rule – Deny the deduction in payer jurisdiction

If the parent jurisdiction does not neutralise the mismatch, the payer jurisdiction will deny the deduction for such payment to the extent it gives rise to a DD outcome.

(c) Mismatch does not arise to extent the deduction is set off against dual inclusion income

No mismatch will arise to the extent that a deduction is set-off against income that is included as ordinary income under the laws of both the parent and the payer jurisdictions (i.e. dual inclusion income).

(d) Treatment of excess deduction

(i) Any deduction that exceeds the amount of dual inclusion income (the excess deduction) may be eligible to be set-off against dual inclusion income in another period.

(ii) In order to prevent stranded losses, the excess deduction may be allowed to the extent that the taxpayer can establish, to the satisfaction of the tax administration, that the deduction in the other jurisdiction cannot be set off against any income of any person under the laws of the other jurisdiction.

2 Rule only applies to deductible payments made by a hybrid payer

A person will be a treated as a hybrid payer in respect of a payment that is deductible under the laws of the payer jurisdiction where:

Recommendation 6. *(Cont.)*

(a) the payer is a not a resident of the payer jurisdiction and the payment triggers a duplicate deduction for that payer (or a related person) under the laws of the jurisdiction where the payer is resident (the parent jurisdiction); or

(b) the payer is resident in the payer jurisdiction and the payment triggers a duplicate deduction for an investor in that payer (or a related person) under the laws of the other jurisdiction (the parent jurisdiction).

3 Rule only applies to payments that result in a hybrid mismatch

A payment results in a hybrid mismatch where the deduction for the payment may be set-off, under the laws of the payer jurisdiction, against income that is not dual inclusion income.

4 Scope

(a) There is no limitation on scope in respect of the recommended response.

(b) The defensive rule only applies if the parties to the mismatch are in the same control group or where the mismatch arises under a structured arrangement and the taxpayer is party to that structured arrangement.

Recommended hybrid mismatch rule for deductible payments by a dual-resident

100. This section sets out recommendations for the design of hybrid mismatch rules to prevent a deductible payment made by a dual resident entity triggering a duplicate deduction under the laws of another jurisdiction. The example below illustrates this kind of mismatch can be engineered through such dual-consolidation structures.

Figure 3.2 Dual Consolidated Companies

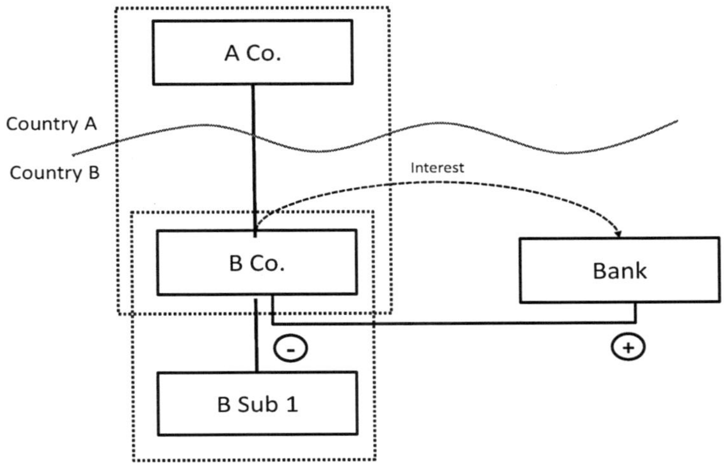

101. In the example illustrated in Figure 3.2, A Co (a company incorporated and tax resident in Country A) holds all the shares in B Co (a company incorporated in Country B but tax resident in both Country A and Country B). B Co owns all the shares in B Sub 1 (a company tax resident and incorporated in Country B). B Co is consolidated, for tax purposes, with both A Co (under Country A law) and B Sub 1 (under B Country Law).

102. As with the example in Figure 3.1 above, B Co borrows from a bank and pays interest on the loan. B Co derives no other income. Because B Co is resident in both Country A and Country B it is subject to tax on its worldwide income in both jurisdictions on a net basis and can surrender any net loss under the tax consolidation regimes of both countries to other resident companies. The ability to "surrender" the tax benefit through the consolidation regime in both countries allows the two deductions for the interest expense to be set-off against separate income arising in Country A and Country B.

Recommended rule

103. The recommended hybrid mismatch rule isolates the hybrid element in the structure by identifying a deductible payment made by a dual resident in the payer jurisdiction and the corresponding "duplicate deduction" generated in the other jurisdiction where the payer is resident. The primary response is that the deduction cannot be claimed in the payer jurisdiction to the extent it exceeds the payer's dual inclusion income (income brought into account for tax purposes under the laws of both jurisdictions). As both jurisdictions will apply the primary response there is no need for a defensive rule.

104. As with other structures that generate DD outcomes the excess deductions can be offset against dual inclusion income in another period. In order to prevent stranded losses, it is recommended that excess duplicate deductions should be allowed to the extent that the taxpayer can establish, to the satisfaction of the tax administration, that the deduction cannot be set-off against the income of any person under the laws of the other jurisdiction.

105. Recommended language for a domestic law hybrid mismatch rule is set out in the box below:

Recommendation 7.
Dual resident payer rule

The following rule should apply to a dual resident that makes a payment that is deductible under the laws of both jurisdictions where the payer is resident and that DD outcome results in a hybrid mismatch (as defined in paragraph 3 below).

1 Neutralise the mismatch to the extent the payment gives rise to DD Outcome

(a) Response - Deny the deduction in the resident jurisdiction

Each resident jurisdiction will deny a deduction for such payment to the extent it gives rise to a DD outcome.

(b) Rule does not apply to extent the deduction is set off against dual inclusion income

No mismatch will arise to the extent that the deduction is set-off against income that is included as ordinary income under the laws of both jurisdictions (dual inclusion income).

(c) Treatment of excess deduction

(i) Any deduction that exceeds the amount of dual inclusion income (the excess deduction) may be eligible to be set-off against dual inclusion income in another period.

(ii) In order to prevent stranded losses, the excess deduction may be allowed to the extent that the taxpayer can establish, to the satisfaction of the tax administration, that the excess deduction cannot be set off against any income under the laws of the other jurisdiction that is not dual inclusion income.

Recommendation 7. *(Cont.)*

2 Rule only applies to deductible payments made by a dual resident

A taxpayer will be a dual resident if it is resident for tax purposes under the laws of two or more jurisdictions.

3 Rule only applies to payments that result in a hybrid mismatch

A deduction for a payment results in a hybrid mismatch where the deduction for the payment may be set-off, under the laws of the other jurisdiction, against income that is not dual inclusion income.

Chapter 4

Arrangements that produce indirect D/NI outcomes

Recommended rule for indirect D/NI outcomes

106. The effect of a hybrid mismatch that arises between two jurisdictions can be shifted (or imported) into another jurisdiction through the use of a plain-vanilla financial instrument such as an ordinary loan. Imported mismatches rely on the absence of effective hybrid mismatch rules in the investor and intermediary jurisdictions in order to generate the mismatch in tax outcomes which can then be imported into the payer jurisdiction. A simple example of an imported mismatch structure is illustrated in Figure 4.1.

Figure 4.1 Importing Mismatch from Hybrid Financial Instrument

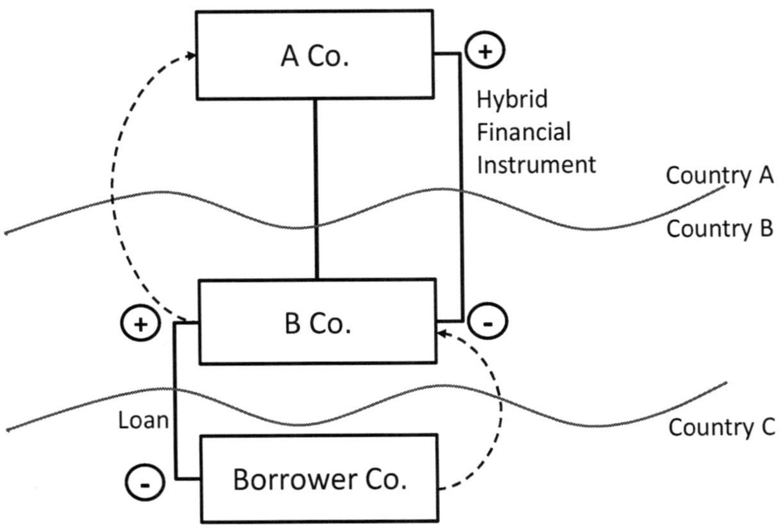

107. Under this structure, B Co is a wholly-owned subsidiary of A Co. A Co lends money to B Co using a hybrid financial instrument. The payments under this instrument will be exempt from tax under the laws of Country A, while being deductible under the laws of Country B. Borrower Co borrows money from B Co. Interest payable under the loan is deductible under the laws of Borrower Co's jurisdiction (Country C) and included in income by B Co under Country B law. The result of this structure is an indirect D/NI outcome between Countries A and C. Country B's tax revenue is unaffected as the income and deductions of B Co offset each other.

Recommended rule

108. The most reliable protection against imported mismatches will be for all jurisdictions to introduce rules recommended in this Report. Such rules will address the effect of the hybrid mismatch arrangement in the jurisdiction where it arises, and therefore prevent the effect of such mismatch being imported into a third jurisdiction. In order to protect the integrity of the recommendations, however, this Report further recommends the adoption of a linking rule that denies a deduction for such payments to the extent they give rise to an indirect D/NI outcome. This Report only recommends the adoption of the primary response of denying the payer a deduction for payments made under an imported mismatch arrangement.

109. A payment will be treated as made under an imported mismatch arrangement if the payee offsets a deduction under a hybrid mismatch arrangement against the income from such payment. The rules applicable to timing differences under the other hybrid mismatch rules are incorporated into the imported mismatch rule by reference.

110. This rule only applies if the parties to the mismatch (A Co, B Co and Borrower Co in the above example) are in the same control group or where the payment is made under a structured arrangement and the taxpayer is party to that structured arrangement.

111. Public submissions raise concerns as to the potential impact of the imported mismatch rule on non-structured arrangements entered into by a taxpayer. Further work will be done to better understand whether there are any situations where it would be disproportionate and unduly burdensome to require the taxpayer to apply the rule and, if so, whether the application of the hybrid mismatch rule to such arrangements should be restricted or better targeted. In addition, further work will be undertaken regarding the implementation of this rule so that it is clear, administrable and avoids double taxation.

112. Recommended language for a domestic law hybrid mismatch rule is set out in the box below:

Recommendation 8.
Imported Mismatch Rule

An imported mismatch arrangement is an arrangement that gives rise to a hybrid mismatch under the laws of another jurisdiction and the effect of that mismatch is imported into the payer jurisdiction by offsetting the deduction under that hybrid mismatch arrangement against the income from the payment.

1 Neutralise the mismatch to extent payment gives rise to DD Outcome

(a) Response - Deny the Deduction

The payer jurisdiction will deny a deduction for a payment made under an imported mismatch arrangement to the extent that the hybrid deduction is set-off against the payment in the payee jurisdiction.

2 Rule only applies to payments that are set-off against a deduction under the imported mismatch arrangement

(a) A hybrid deduction is a deduction for:

(i) a payment under a financial instrument that results in a hybrid mismatch;

(ii) a disregarded payment made by a hybrid payer that results in a hybrid mismatch;

(iii) a payment made to a reverse hybrid that results in a hybrid mismatch;

(iv) a payment made by a hybrid payer or dual resident that triggers a duplicate deduction resulting in a hybrid mismatch; or

(v) a payment made to a person that offsets the income from such payment against a deduction under an imported mismatch arrangement.

3 Scope

The rule applies if the taxpayer is in the same control group as the parties to the imported mismatch arrangement or where the payment is made under a structured arrangement and the taxpayer is party to that structured arrangement.

Chapter 5

Implementation

Recommendations on implementation and co-ordination

113. The recommendations set out in this Report have been developed in light of the design principles set out in this Chapter. In particular, the recommendations are intended to operate as a comprehensive and coherent package of measures to neutralise mismatches that arise from the use of hybrid instruments and entities, without imposing undue burdens on taxpayers and tax administrations. Jurisdictions that implement these rules should seek to do so in a way that achieves outcomes that are consistent with the design principles.

114. The recommendations also create a framework for jurisdictions to co-ordinate their response to hybrid mismatches. Co-operation between tax administrations will therefore be needed to ensure that jurisdictions apply these rules consistently and effectively. Whilst recognising that jurisdictions have different legislative timetables and processes, the OECD and G20 will consider the extent to which it is possible to co-ordinate the timing of the implementation of the rules and whether a number of jurisdictions can agree to introduce provisions that are effective from a common date. Additionally the OECD and G20 will provide written guidance on the application of the recommendations that will take the form of a Commentary to be published no later than September 2015, which will provide further explanation and examples detailing how the rules will operate in practice and will include transitional rules setting out how the rules will apply if there are differing dates of implementation.

115. Jurisdictions and taxpayers applying the rules will need to understand how a financial instrument or entity is treated in another jurisdiction. In addition, they will need to know whether or not hybrid rules are in operation in a counterparty jurisdiction. To this end, work will be done to share information between jurisdictions and with taxpayers.

116. Jurisdictions agree that the recommendations in this Report should also be subject to ongoing review to ensure that they are operating effectively and consistently with the other recommendations adopted as part of the BEPS Action items, particularly those under Actions 3,[1] 4,[2] and 12.[3]

117. It is also recognised that the outputs from other Actions may have an effect on the intended outcomes under the hybrid mismatch rules. For example if a jurisdiction were to adopt a broad interest limitation measure; limiting the amount of interest that is deductible by a domestic group to a proportion of the interest paid by the worldwide group, it may no longer need the hybrid financial instrument rule to adjust the tax outcomes for members of a controlled group (although it may still need rules to tackle structured arrangements and financial instruments that are entered into outside of the group).

118. Recommendations as to the implementation and co-ordination of the recommendations are set out below.

Recommendation 9.
Implementation and Co-ordination

1 Design principles

The hybrid mismatch rules have been designed to maximise the following outcomes:

(a) neutralise the mismatch rather than reverse the tax benefit that arises under the laws of the jurisdiction;

(b) be comprehensive;

(c) apply automatically;

(d) avoid double taxation through rule co-ordination;

(e) minimise the disruption to existing domestic law;

(f) be clear and transparent in their operation;

(g) provide sufficient flexibility for the rule to be incorporated into the laws of each jurisdiction;

(h) be workable for taxpayers and keep compliance costs to a minimum; and

(i) minimise the administrative burden on tax authorities.

Jurisdictions that implement these recommendations into domestic law should do so in a manner intended to preserve these design principles.

Recommendation 9. ***(Cont.)***

2 Implementation and co-ordination

Jurisdictions should co-operate on measures to ensure these recommendations are implemented and applied consistently and effectively. These measures should include:

(a) the development of agreed guidance on the recommendations;

(b) co-ordination of the implementation of the recommendations (including timing);

(c) development of transitional rules (without any presumption as to grandfathering of existing arrangements);

(d) review of the effective and consistent implementation of the recommendations;

(e) exchange of information on the jurisdiction treatment of hybrid financial instruments and hybrid entities;

(f) endeavouring to make relevant information available to taxpayers (including reasonable endeavours by the OECD); and

(g) consideration of the interaction of the recommendations with other Actions under the BEPS Action Plan including Actions 3 and 4.

Notes

1. See Action 3 – Strengthen CFC rules (OECD, 2013), pp. 16-17.

2. See Action 4 – Limit base erosion via interest deductions and other financial payments (OECD, 2013), p. 17.

3. See Action 12 – Require taxpayers to disclose their aggressive tax planning arrangements (OECD, 2013), pp. 22-23.

Bibliography

OECD (2013), *Action Plan on Base Erosion and Profit Shifting*, OECD Publishing.
http://dx.doi.org/10.1787/9789264202719-en.

Chapter 6

Definitions in relation to scope

119. As discussed at paragraph 21, overly broad hybrid mismatch rules may be difficult to apply and administer. Accordingly, these recommendations have adopted a bottom-up approach to the scope of the hybrid mismatch rules. Specifically this approach scopes in hybrid financial instruments held by related parties (including persons acting together) and other mismatch arrangements where the parties to the mismatch are members of the same controlled group. A person is treated as holding, for the purposes of the related party and control tests, any investments held by an investor that is acting together with that person. The hybrid mismatch rules also apply to any person who is party to a "structured" arrangement that has been designed to produce a mismatch.

Definition of structured arrangement

120. Jurisdictions should incorporate definitions into domestic law that are consistent with the definitions set out in this box to establish the scope of the hybrid mismatch rules.

Recommendation 10.
Definition of Structured Arrangement

1 General Definition

Structured arrangement is any arrangement where the hybrid mismatch is priced into the terms of the arrangement or the facts and circumstances (including the terms) of the arrangement indicate that it has been designed to produce a hybrid mismatch.

Recommendation 10. *(Cont.)*

2 Specific Examples of Structured Arrangements

Facts and circumstances that indicate that an arrangement has been designed to produce a hybrid mismatch include any of the following:

(a) an arrangement that is designed, or is part of a plan, to create a hybrid mismatch;

(b) an arrangement that incorporates a term, step or transaction used in order to create a hybrid mismatch;

(c) an arrangement that is marketed, in whole or in part, as a tax-advantaged product where some or all of the tax advantage derives from the hybrid mismatch;

(d) an arrangement that is primarily marketed to taxpayers in a jurisdiction where the hybrid mismatch arises;

(e) an arrangement that contains features that alter the terms under the arrangement, including the return, in the event that the hybrid mismatch is no longer available; or

(f) an arrangement that would produce a negative return absent the hybrid mismatch.

3 When taxpayer not a party to a Structured Arrangement

A taxpayer will not be treated as a party to a structured arrangement if neither the taxpayer nor any member of the same control group could reasonably have been expected to be aware of the hybrid mismatch and did not share in the value of the tax benefit resulting from the hybrid mismatch.

Definition of related person, control group and acting together

121. Jurisdictions should incorporate definitions into domestic law that are consistent with the definitions set out in this box to establish the scope of the hybrid mismatch rules.

Recommendation 11.
Definition of Related Persons, Control Group and Acting Together

1 *General Definition*

(a) Two persons are related if they are in the same control group or the first person has a 25% or greater investment in the second person or there is a third person that holds a 25% or greater investment in both.

(b) Two persons are in the same control group if:

- they are consolidated for accounting purposes;
- the first person has an investment that provides that person with effective control of the second person or there is a third person that holds investments which provides that person with effective control over both persons;
- the first person has a 50% or greater investment in the second person or there is a third person that holds a 50% or greater investment in both; or
- they can be regarded as associated enterprises under Article 9.

(c) A person will be treated as holding a percentage investment in another person if that person holds directly or indirectly through an investment in other persons, a percentage of the voting rights of that person or of the value of any equity interests of that person.

2 *Aggregation of interests*

For the purposes of the related party rules a person who acts together with another person in respect of ownership or control of any voting rights or equity interests will be treated as owning or controlling all the voting rights and equity interests of that person.

3 *Acting together*

Two persons will be treated as acting together in respect of ownership or control of any voting rights or equity interests if:

(a) they are members of the same family;

(b) one person regularly acts in accordance with the wishes of the other person in respect of ownership or control of such rights or interests;

(c) they have entered into an arrangement that has material impact on the value or control of any such rights or interests; or

Recommendation 11. *(Cont.)*

(d) the ownership or control of any such rights or interests are managed by the same person or group of persons. In respect of any taxpayer that is a collective investment vehicle if the investment manager can establish to the satisfaction of the tax authority from the terms of the investment mandate and the circumstances in which the investment was made, that two funds were not acting together in respect of the investment then the interest held by those funds should not be aggregated under this sub-paragraph of the acting together test.

Chapter 7

Key terms

Agreed definitions

122. Jurisdictions should incorporate definitions into domestic law that are consistent with the definitions set out in this chapter for the purpose of these recommendations to ensure consistency in the application of the recommendations.

Recommendation 12.
Other Definitions

Accrued income	Accrued income, in relation to any payee and any investor, means income of the payee that has accrued for the benefit of that investor.
Arrangement	Arrangement refers to an agreement, contract, scheme, plan, or understanding, whether enforceable or not, including all steps and transactions by which it is carried into effect. An arrangement may be part of a wider arrangement, it may be a single arrangement, or it may be comprised of a number of arrangements.
Collective investment vehicle	Collective investment vehicle means a collective investment vehicle as defined in paragraph 4 of the Granting of Treaty Benefits with Respect to the Income of Collective Investment Vehicles (2010, OECD)
Constitution	Constitution, in relation to any person, means the rules governing the relationship between the person and its owners and includes articles of association or incorporation.
D/NI outcome	A payment gives rise to a D/NI outcome to the extent the payment is deductible under the laws of the payer jurisdiction but is not included in ordinary income by any person in the payee jurisdiction or by any related investor in the payee.

Recommendation 12. *(Cont.)*

	A D/NI outcome is not generally impacted by questions of timing in the recognition of payments or differences in the way jurisdictions measure the value of money. In some circumstances however a timing mismatch will be considered permanent if the taxpayer cannot establish to the satisfaction of a tax authority that a payment will be brought into account within a defined period.
DD outcome	A payment gives rise to a DD outcome if the payment is deductible under the laws of more than one jurisdiction.
Deduction	Deduction (including deductible), in respect of a payment, means that, after a proper determination of the character and treatment of the payment under the laws of the payer jurisdiction, the payment is taken into account as a deduction or equivalent tax relief under the laws of that jurisdiction in calculating the taxpayer's net income.
Director	Director, in relation to any person, means any person who has the power under the constitution to manage and control that person and includes a trustee;
Distribution	Distribution, in relation to any person, means a payment of profits or gains by that person to any owner.
Dual inclusion income	Dual inclusion income, in the case of both deductible payments and disregarded payments, refers to any item of income that is included as ordinary income under the laws of the jurisdictions where the mismatch has arisen.
Equity interests	Equity interests means any interest in any person that includes an entitlement to an Equity return.
Equity return	Equity return means an entitlement to profits or eligibility to participate in distributions of any person and, in respect of any arrangement is a return on that arrangement that is economically equivalent to a distribution or a return of profits or where it is reasonable to assume, after consideration of the terms of the arrangement, that the return is calculated by reference to distributions or profits.
Establishment jurisdiction	Establishment jurisdiction, in relation to any person, means the jurisdiction where that person is incorporated or otherwise established.

Recommendation 12. *(Cont.)*

Family	A person (A) is a member of the same family as another person (B) if B is: • the spouse or civil partner of A, • a 'relative' of A (brother, sister, ancestor or lineal descendant), • the spouse or civil partner of a relative of A, • a relative of A's spouse or civil partner, • the spouse or civil partner of a relative of A's spouse or civil partner. • an adopted relative.
Financing return	Financing return, in respect of any arrangement is a return on that arrangement that is economically equivalent to interest or where it is reasonable to assume, after consideration of the terms of the arrangement, that the return is calculated by reference to the time value of money provided under the arrangement.
Hybrid mismatch	A hybrid mismatch is defined in paragraph 3 in Recommendations 1, 3, 4, 6 and 7 for the purposes of those Recommendations.
Included in ordinary income	A payment will be treated as included in ordinary income to the extent that, after a proper determination of the character and treatment of the payment under the laws of the relevant jurisdiction, the payment has been incorporated as ordinary income into a calculation of the payee's income under the law of the relevant jurisdiction. [A payment will be treated as included in ordinary income to the extent the taxpayer can establish, to the satisfaction of the tax administration, that the payment has been treated as ordinary income of a related party investor under an offshore investment regime that taxes the investor on such income on substantially the same basis as the payment would have been taxed if it had been made directly to investor.]
Investor	Investor, in relation to any person, means any person directly or indirectly holding voting rights or equity interests in that person.

Recommendation 12. *(Cont.)*

Investor jurisdiction	Investor jurisdiction is any jurisdiction where the investor is a taxpayer.
Mismatch	A mismatch is a DD outcome or a D/NI outcome and includes an expected mismatch.
Money	Money includes money in any form, anything that is convertible into money and any provision that would be paid for at arm's length.
Offshore investment regime	An offshore investment regime includes controlled foreign company and foreign investment fund rules and any other rules that require the investor's accrued income to be included on a current basis under the laws of the investor's jurisdiction.
Ordinary income	Ordinary income means income that is subject to tax at the taxpayer's full marginal rate and does not benefit from any exemption, exclusion, credit or other tax relief applicable to particular categories of payments (such as indirect credits for underlying tax on income of the payer). Income is considered subject to tax at the taxpayer's full marginal rate notwithstanding that the tax on the inclusion is reduced by a credit or other tax relief granted by the payee jurisdiction for withholding tax or other taxes imposed by the payer jurisdiction on the payment itself.
Payee	Payee means any person who receives a payment under an arrangement including through a permanent establishment of the payee.
Payee jurisdiction	Payee jurisdiction is any jurisdiction where the payee is a taxpayer.
Payer	Payer means any person who makes a payment under an arrangement including through a permanent establishment of the payer.
Payer jurisdiction	Payer jurisdiction is any jurisdiction where the payer is a taxpayer.
Payment	Payment includes any amount capable of being paid including (but not limited to) a distribution, credit, debit, accrual of money but it does not extend to payments that are only deemed to be made for tax purposes and that do not involve the creation of economic rights between parties.

Recommendation 12. ***(Cont.)***

	In respect of a hybrid transfer, payment includes the aggregate amounts paid under the arrangement that give rise to the D/NI outcome.
Person	Person includes any natural or legal person or unincorporated body of persons and a trust.
Taxpayer	Taxpayer, in respect of any jurisdiction, means any person who is subject to tax in that jurisdiction whether as a resident or by virtue of applicable source rules (such as maintaining a permanent establishment in that jurisdiction).
Trust	Trust includes any person who is a trustee of a trust acting in that capacity.
Voting rights	Voting rights means the right to participate in any decision-making concerning a distribution, a change to the constitution or the appointment of a director.

Part II

Recommendation on treaty issues

Introduction

123. Part II of this Report complements Part I and deals with the parts of Action 2 that indicate that the outputs of the work on that action item may include "changes to the OECD Model Tax Convention to ensure that hybrid instruments and entities (as well as dual resident entities) are not used to obtain the benefits of treaties unduly" and that stress that "[s]pecial attention should be given to the interaction between possible changes to domestic law and the provisions of the OECD Model Tax Convention."[1]

124. This part first examines treaty issues related to dual-resident entities (Chapter 8). It then includes a proposal for a new treaty provision dealing with transparent entities (Chapter 9). Chapter 10 addresses the issue of the interaction between the recommendations included in Part I of this Report and the provisions of tax treaties.

125. At the outset, it should be noted that a number of proposals resulting from the work on Action 6 (Preventing Treaty Abuse), which were included in a discussion draft released on 14 March 2014 (Treaty Abuse Discussion Draft)[2], may play an important role in ensuring "that hybrid instruments and entities (as well as dual resident entities) are not used to obtain the benefits of treaties unduly". The following proposals included in that other discussion draft may be of particular relevance:

- Limitation-on-benefits rules;
- Rule aimed at arrangements one of the main purposes of which is to obtain treaty benefits;
- Rule aimed at dividend transfer transactions (*i.e.* to subject the lower rate of tax provided by Art. 10(2)*a*) or by a treaty provision applicable to pension funds to a minimum shareholding period);
- Rule concerning a Contracting State's right to tax its own residents;
- Anti-abuse rule for permanent establishments situated in third States.

Notes

1. See Action 2 – Neutralise the effects of hybrid mismatch arrangements (OECD 2013), pp. 15-16.

2. Release of the Discussion draft on Action 6 (Prevent Treaty Abuse) of the BEPS Action Plan, March 2014, www.oecd.org/tax/treaties/discussion-draft-action-6-prevent-treaty-abuse.htm.

Bibliography

OECD (2013), *Action Plan on Base Erosion and Profit Shifting*, OECD Publishing. http://dx.doi.org/10.1787/9789264202719-en

Chapter 8

Dual–resident entities

126. Action 2 refers expressly to possible changes to the OECD Model Tax Convention to ensure that dual resident entities are not used to obtain the benefits of treaties unduly.

127. The change to Art. 4(3) of the OECD Model Tax Convention that is recommended as part of the work on Action 6 will address some of the BEPS concerns related to the issue of dual-resident entities by providing that cases of dual treaty residence would be solved on a case-by-case basis rather than on the basis of the current rule based on place of effective management of entities, which creates a potential for tax avoidance in some countries. The new version of Art. 4(3) that is recommended reads as follows:

> *3. Where by reason of the provisions of paragraph 1 a person other than an individual is a resident of both Contracting States, the competent authorities of the Contracting States shall endeavour to determine by mutual agreement the Contracting State of which such person shall be deemed to be a resident for the purposes of the Convention, having regard to its place of effective management, the place where it is incorporated or otherwise constituted and any other relevant factors. In the absence of such agreement, such person shall not be entitled to any relief or exemption from tax provided by this Convention except to the extent and in such manner as may be agreed upon by the competent authorities of the Contracting States.*

128. This change, however, will not address all BEPS concerns related to dual-resident entities. It will not, for instance, address avoidance strategies resulting from an entity being a resident of a given State under that State's domestic law whilst, at the same time, being a resident of another State under a tax treaty concluded by the

first State, thereby allowing that entity to benefit from the advantages applicable to residents under domestic law without being subject to reciprocal obligations (*e.g.* being able to shift its foreign losses to another resident company under a domestic law group relief system while claiming treaty protection against taxation of its foreign profits). That issue arises from a mismatch between the treaty and domestic law concepts of residence and since the treaty concept of residence cannot simply be aligned on the domestic law concept of residence of each Contracting State without creating situations where an entity would be a resident of the two States for the purposes of the treaty, the solution to these avoidance strategies must be found in domestic law. Whilst such avoidance strategies may be addressed through domestic general anti-abuse rules, States for which this is a potential problem may wish to consider inserting into their domestic law a rule, already found in the domestic law of some States,[1] according to which an entity that is considered to be a resident of another State under a tax treaty will be deemed not to be a resident under domestic law.

129. Also, the change to Art. 4(3) will not address BEPS concerns that arise from dual-residence where no treaty is involved. Figure 3.2 of Part I of the Report illustrates a dual consolidation structure where BEPS concerns arise from the fact that two States consider the same entity as a resident to which each country applies its consolidation regime. In such a case, the same BEPS concerns arise whether or not there is a tax treaty between the two States, which indicates that the solution to such a case needs to be found in domestic laws. It should be noted, however, that if a treaty existed between the two States and the domestic law of each State included the provision referred to in the preceding paragraph, the entity would likely be a resident under the domestic law of only one State, i.e. the State of which it would be a resident under the treaty.

Note

1. See subsection 250(5) of the *Income Tax Act* of Canada and section 18 of the *Corporation Tax Act* 2009 of the United Kingdom.

Bibliography

Parliament of the United Kingdom (2009), *Corporation Tax Act 2009*, United Kingdom. Available at: www.legislation.gov.uk/ukpga/2009/4/contents

Chapter 9

Treaty provision on transparent entities

130. The 1999 OECD report on *The Application of the OECD Model Tax Convention to Partnerships* (the Partnership Report)[1] contains an extensive analysis of the application of treaty provisions to partnerships, including in situations where there is a mismatch in the tax treatment of the partnership. The main conclusions of the Partnership Report, which have been included in the Commentary of the OECD Model Tax Convention, seek to ensure that the provisions of tax treaties produce appropriate results when applied to partnerships, in particular in the case of a partnership that constitutes a hybrid entity.

131. The Partnership Report, however, did not expressly address the application of tax treaties to entities other than partnerships. In order to address that issue, as well as the fact that some countries have found it difficult to apply the conclusions of the Partnership Report, it is proposed to include in the OECD Model Tax Convention the following provision and Commentary, which will ensure that income of transparent entities is treated, for the purposes of the Convention, in accordance with the principles of the Partnership Report. This will not only ensure that the benefits of tax treaties are granted in appropriate cases but also that these benefits are not granted where neither Contracting State treats, under its domestic law, the income of an entity as the income of one of its residents.

Replace Article 1 of the Model Tax Convention by the following (additions to the existing text appear in ***bold italics****):*

Article 1

PERSONS COVERED

1. This Convention shall apply to persons who are residents of one or both of the Contracting States.

2. For the purposes of this Convention, income derived by or through an entity or arrangement that is treated as wholly or partly fiscally transparent under the tax law of either Contracting State shall be considered to be income of a resident of a Contracting State but only to the extent that the income is treated, for purposes of taxation by that State, as the income of a resident of that State. [In no case shall the provisions of this paragraph be construed so as to restrict in any way a Contracting State's right to tax the residents of that State.][2]

Add the following paragraphs 26.3 to 26.16 to the Commentary on Article 1 (other consequential changes to the Commentary on Article 1 would be required):

Paragraph 2

26.3 This paragraph addresses the situation of the income of entities or arrangements that one or both Contracting States treat as wholly or partly fiscally transparent for tax purposes. The provisions of the paragraph ensure that income of such entities or arrangements is treated, for the purposes of the Convention, in accordance with the principles reflected in the 1999 report of the Committee on Fiscal Affairs entitled "The Application of the OECD Model Tax Convention to Partnerships".[3] ***That Report therefore provides guidance and examples on how the provision should be interpreted and applied in various situations.***

26.4 The Report, however, dealt exclusively with partnerships and whilst the Committee recognised that many of the principles included in the Report could also apply with respect to other non-corporate entities, it expressed the intention to examine the application of the Model Tax Convention to these other entities at a later stage. As indicated in paragraph 37 of the Report, the Committee was particularly concerned with "cases where domestic tax laws create intermediary situations where a partnership is partly treated as a taxable unit and partly disregarded for tax purposes." According to the Report

> ***Whilst this may create practical difficulties with respect to a very limited number of partnerships, it is a more important problem in the case of other entities such as trusts. For this reason, the Committee decided to deal with this issue in the context of follow-up work to this report.***

26.5 Paragraph 2 addresses this particular situation by referring to entities that are "wholly or partly" treated as fiscally transparent.

Thus, the paragraph not only serves to confirm the conclusions of the Partnership Report but also extends the application of these conclusions to situations that were not directly covered by the Report (subject to the application of specific provisions dealing with collective investment vehicles, see paragraphs 6.17 to 6.34 above).

26.6 The paragraph not only ensures that the benefits of the Convention are granted in appropriate cases but also ensures that these benefits are not granted where neither Contracting State treats, under its domestic law, the income of an entity or arrangement as the income of one of its residents. The paragraph therefore confirms the conclusions of the Report in such a case (see, for example, example 3 of the Report). Also, as recognised in the Report, States should not be expected to grant the benefits of a bilateral tax convention in cases where they cannot verify whether a person is truly entitled to these benefits. Thus, if an entity is established in a jurisdiction from which a Contracting State cannot obtain tax information, that State would need to be provided with all the necessary information in order to be able to grant the benefits of the Convention. In such a case, the Contracting State might well decide to use the refund mechanism for the purposes of applying the benefits of the Convention even though it normally applies these benefits at the time of the payment of the relevant income. In most cases, however, it will be possible to obtain the relevant information and to apply the benefits of the Convention at the time the income is received (see for example paragraphs 6.29 to 6.31 above which discuss a similar issue in the context of collective investment vehicles).

26.7 The following example illustrates the application of the paragraph:

> *Example: State A and State B have concluded a treaty identical to the Model Tax Convention. State A considers that an entity established in State B is a company and taxes that entity on interest that it receives from a debtor resident in State A. Under the domestic law of State B, however, the entity is treated as a partnership and the two members in that entity, who share equally all its income, are each taxed on half of the interest. One of the members is a resident of State B and the other one is a resident of a country with which States A and B do not have a treaty. The paragraph provides that in such case, half of the interest shall be considered, for the purposes of Article 11, to be income of a resident of State B.*

26.8 The reference to "income derived by or through an entity or arrangement" has a broad meaning and covers any income that is earned by or through an entity or arrangement, regardless of the view taken by each Contracting State as to who derives that income for domestic tax purposes and regardless of whether or not that entity or arrangement has legal personality or constitutes a person as defined in subparagraph 1 a) of Article 3. It would cover, for example, income of any partnership or trust that one or both of the Contracting States treats as wholly or partly fiscally transparent. Also, as illustrated in example 2 of the Report, it does not matter where the entity or arrangement is established: the paragraph applies to an entity established in a third State to the extent that, under the domestic tax law of one of the Contracting States, the entity is treated as wholly or partly fiscally transparent and income of that entity is attributed to a resident of that State.

26.9 The word "income" must be given the wide meaning that it has for the purposes of the Convention and therefore applies to the various items of income that are covered by Chapter III of the Convention (Taxation of Income), including, for example, profits of an enterprise and capital gains.

26.10 The concept of "fiscally transparent" used in the paragraph refers to situations where, under the domestic law of a Contracting State, the income (or part thereof) of the entity or arrangement is not taxed at the level of the entity or the arrangement but at the level of the persons who have an interest in that entity or arrangement. This will normally be the case where the amount of tax payable on a share of the income of an entity or arrangement is determined separately in relation to the personal characteristics of the person who is entitled to that share so that the tax will depend on whether that person is taxable or not, on the other income that the person has, on the personal allowances to which the person is entitled and on the tax rate applicable to that person; also, the character and source, as well as the timing of the realisation, of the income for tax purposes will not be affected by the fact that it has been earned through the entity or arrangement. The fact that the income is computed at the level of the entity or arrangement before the share is allocated to the person will not affect that result.[4] States wishing to clarify the definition of "fiscally transparent" in their bilateral conventions are free to include a definition of that term based on the above explanations.

26.11 In the case of an entity or arrangement which is treated as partly fiscally transparent under the domestic law of one of the

Contracting States, only part of the income of the entity or arrangement might be taxed at the level of the persons who have an interest in that entity or arrangement as described in the preceding paragraph whilst the rest would remain taxable at the level of the entity or arrangement. This, for example, is how some trusts and limited liability partnerships are treated in some countries (i.e. in some countries, the part of the income derived through a trust that is distributed to beneficiaries is taxed in the hands of these beneficiaries whilst the part of that income that is accumulated is taxed in the hands of the trust or trustees; similarly, in some countries, income derived through a limited partnership is taxed in the hands of the general partner as regards that partner's share of that income but is considered to be the income of the limited partnership as regards the limited partners' share of the income). To the extent that the entity or arrangement qualifies as a resident of a Contracting State, the paragraph will ensure that the benefits of the treaty also apply to the share of the income that is attributed to the entity or arrangement under the domestic law of that State (subject to any anti-abuse provision such as a limitation-on-benefits rule).

26.12 As with other provisions of the Convention, the provision applies separately to each item of income of the entity or arrangement. Assume, for example, that the document that establishes a trust provides that all dividends received by the trust must be distributed to a beneficiary during the lifetime of that beneficiary but must be accumulated afterwards. If one of the Contracting States considers that, in such a case, the beneficiary is taxable on the dividends distributed to that beneficiary but that the trustees are taxable on the dividends that will be accumulated, the paragraph will apply differently to these two categories of dividends even if both types of dividends are received within the same month.

26.13 By providing that the income to which it applies will be considered to be income of a resident of a Contracting State for the purposes of the Convention, the paragraph ensures that the relevant income is attributed to that resident for the purposes of the application of the various allocative rules of the Convention. Depending on the nature of the income, this will therefore allow the income to be considered, for example, as "income derived by" for the purposes of Articles 6, 13 and 17, "profits of an enterprise" for the purposes of Articles 7, 8 and 9 (see also paragraph 4 of the Commentary on Article 3) or dividends or interest "paid to" for the purposes of Articles 10 and 11. The fact that the income is

considered to be derived by a resident of a Contracting State for the purposes of the Convention also means that where the income constitutes a share of the income of an enterprise in which that resident holds a participation, such income shall be considered to be the income of an enterprise carried on by that resident (e.g. for the purposes of the definition of enterprise of a Contracting State in Article 3 and paragraph 2 of Article 21).

26.14 Whilst the paragraph ensures that the various allocative rules of the Convention are applied to the extent that income of fiscally transparent entities is treated, under domestic law, as income of a resident of a Contracting State, the paragraph does not prejudge the issue of whether the recipient is the beneficial owner of the relevant income. Where, for example, a fiscally transparent partnership receives dividends as an agent or nominee for a person who is not a partner, the fact that the dividend may be considered as income of a resident of a Contracting State under the domestic law of that State will not preclude the State of source from considering that neither the partnership nor the partners are the beneficial owners of the dividend.

26.15 The paragraph only applies for the purposes of the Convention and does not, therefore, require a Contracting State to change the way in which it attributes income or characterises entities for the purposes of its domestic law. In the example in paragraph 26.7 above, whilst paragraph 2 provides that half of the interest shall be considered, for the purposes of Article 11, to be income of a resident of State B, this will only affect the maximum amount of tax that State A will be able to collect on the interest and will not change the fact that State A's tax will be payable by the entity. Thus, assuming that the domestic law of State A provides for a 30 per cent withholding tax on the interest, the effect of paragraph 2 will simply be to reduce the amount of tax that State A will collect on the interest (so that half of the interest would be taxed at 30 per cent and half at 10 per cent under the treaty between States A and B) and will not change the fact that the entity is the relevant taxpayer for the purposes of State A's domestic law. Also, the provision does not deal exhaustively with all treaty issues that may arise from the legal nature of certain entities and arrangements and may therefore need to be supplemented by other provisions to address such issues (such as a provision confirming that a trust may qualify as a resident of a Contracting State despite the fact that, under the trust law of many countries, a trust does not constitute a "person").

[26.16 The last sentence of the paragraph clarifies that the paragraph is not intended to restrict in any way a State's right to tax its own residents. This conclusion is consistent with the way in which tax treaties have been interpreted with respect to partnerships (see paragraph 6.1 above). That sentence does not, however, restrict the obligation to provide relief of double taxation that is imposed on a Contracting State by Articles 23 A and 23 B where income of a resident of that State may be taxed by the other State in accordance with the Convention, taking into account the application of the paragraph]. [5]

Notes

1. OECD (1999), *The Application of the OECD Model Tax Convention to Partnerships*, Issues in International Taxation, No. 6, OECD Publishing.
2. Please note that a proposal included in the Treaty Abuse Discussion Draft would make that sentence unnecessary.
3. Reproduced in Volume II of the full-length version of the OECD Model Tax Convention at page R(15)-1.
4. See paragraphs 37-40 of the Partnership Report.
5. A proposal included in the Treaty Abuse Discussion Draft would make that paragraph unnecessary.

Bibliography

OECD (2010), *Model Tax Convention on Income and on Capital: Condensed Version 2010*, OECD Publishing.
http://dx.doi.org/10.1787/mtc_cond-2010-en

OECD (1999), *The Application of the OECD Model Tax Convention to Partnerships*, Issues in International Taxation, No. 6, OECD Publishing.
http://dx.doi.org/10.1787/9789264173316-en

Chapter 10

Interaction between Part I and tax treaties

132. Part I of this Report includes various recommendations for the domestic law treatment of hybrid financial instruments and hybrid entity payments. Since Action 2 provides that "[s]pecial attention should be given to the interaction between possible changes to domestic law and the provisions of the OECD Model Tax Convention", it is necessary to examine treaty issues that may arise from these recommendations.

133. As noted in paragraph the Executive Summary of this Report, Part I will be supported by guidance, in the form of a Commentary to be published no later than September 2015, which will provide further explanation and examples detailing how the rules will operate in practice. Since the detailed explanation of the Working Party No. 11 on Aggressive Tax Planning (WP11) recommendations will only be completed subsequently in 2015, the Working Party No. 1 on Tax Conventions and Related Questions (WP1) conclusions on the treaty aspects of these recommendations will need to be reviewed at that time in order to take account of the additional details that will then be provided.

Rule providing for the denial of deductions

134. Certain of the proposed recommendations in Chapter 2 of Part I include a recommended hybrid mismatch rule under which "the payer jurisdiction will deny a deduction for such payment to the extent it gives rise to a D/NI outcome" to neutralise the effect of hybrid mismatches. This raises the question of whether tax treaties, as currently drafted, would authorise such a denial of deduction. Apart from the rules of Articles 7 and 24, however, the provisions of tax treaties do not govern whether payments are deductible or not and whether they are effectively taxed or not, these being matters of domestic law. The possible application of the provisions of Article 24 with respect to the recommendations set out in Part I of this Report is discussed below; as regards Article 7, paragraph 30 of the Commentary on that Article is particularly relevant:

> *30. Paragraph 2 [of Article 7] determines the profits that are attributable to a permanent establishment for the purposes of the rule in paragraph 1 that allocates taxing rights on these profits. Once the profits that are attributable to a permanent establishment have been determined in accordance with paragraph 2 of Article 7, it is for the domestic law of each Contracting State to determine whether and how such profits should be taxed as long as there is conformity with the requirements of paragraph 2 and the other provisions of the Convention. Paragraph 2 does not deal with the issue of whether expenses are deductible when computing the taxable income of the enterprise in either Contracting State. The conditions for the deductibility of expenses are a matter to be determined by domestic law, subject to the provisions of the Convention and, in particular, paragraph 3 of Article 24 ...*

Defensive rule requiring the inclusion of a payment in ordinary income

135. Certain of the proposed recommendations in Chapter 2 of Part I also include a recommended "defensive" rule under which "[i]f the payer jurisdiction does not neutralise the mismatch then the payee jurisdiction will require such payment to be included in ordinary income to the extent the payment gives rise to a D/NI outcome". The provisions of tax treaties could be implicated if such a rule would seek the imposition of tax on a non-resident whose income would not, under the provisions of the relevant tax treaty, be taxable in that State. The definition of "taxpayer" in the recommendations (Part I, Chapter 7) contemplates the imposition of tax by a jurisdiction only in circumstances where the recipient of the payment is a resident of that jurisdiction or maintains a permanent establishment in that jurisdiction. Since the allocative rules of tax treaties generally do not restrict the taxation rights of the State in such circumstances, any interaction between the recommendation and the provisions of tax treaties will therefore appear to relate primarily to the rules concerning the elimination of double taxation (Articles 23 A and 23 B of the OECD Model Tax Convention).

136. The following two recommendations included in Part I of this Report deal with the elimination of double taxation by the State of residence:

- "In order to prevent D/NI outcomes from arising under a financial instrument, a dividend exemption that is provided for relief against economic double taxation should not be granted under domestic law to the extent the dividend payment is deductible by the payer. Equally, jurisdictions should consider adopting similar restrictions for other types of dividend relief granted to relieve economic double taxation on underlying profits." [Chapter 2, Recommendation 2(1)].

- "In order to prevent duplication of tax credits under a hybrid transfer, any jurisdiction that grants relief for tax withheld at source on a payment made under a hybrid transfer should restrict the benefit of such relief in proportion to the net taxable income of the taxpayer under the arrangement." [Chapter 2, Recommendation 2(2)].

137. As explained below, these recommendations do not appear to raise any issues with respect to the application of Articles 23 A and Articles 23 B of the OECD Model Tax Convention.

Exemption method

138. As regards Articles 23 A (Exemption Method), paragraph 2 of that Article provides that in the case of dividends (covered by Article 10 of the OECD Model Tax Convention), it is the credit method, and not the exemption method, that is applicable. The recommendation that "a dividend exemption that is provided for relief against economic double taxation should not be granted under domestic law to the extent the dividend payment is deductible by the payer" should not, therefore, create problems with respect to bilateral tax treaties that include the wording of Article 23 A.

139. It is recognised, however, that a number of bilateral tax treaties depart from the provisions of Article 23 A and provide for the application of the exemption method with respect to dividends received from foreign companies in which a resident company has a substantial shareholding. This possibility is expressly acknowledged in the OECD Model Tax Convention (see paragraphs 49 to 54 of the Commentary on Articles 23 A and 23 B).

140. Problems arising from the inclusion of the exemption method in tax treaties with respect to items of income that are not taxed in the State of source have long been recognised in the OECD Model Tax Convention (see, for example, paragraph 35 of the Commentary on Articles 23 A and 23 B). Whilst paragraph 4 of Article 23 A[1] may address some situations of hybrid mismatch arrangements where a dividend would otherwise be subject to the exemption method, many tax treaties do not include that provision. At a minimum, therefore, States that wish to follow the recommendation included in Part I of this Report but that enter into tax treaties providing for the application of the exemption method with respect to dividends should consider the inclusion of paragraph 4 of Article 23 A in their tax treaties, although these States should also recognise that the provision will only

provide a partial solution to the problem. A more complete solution that should be considered by these States would be to include in their treaties rules that would expressly allow them to apply the credit method, as opposed to the exemption method, with respect to dividends that are deductible in the payer State. These States may also wish to consider a more general solution to the problems of non-taxation resulting from potential abuses of the exemption method, which would be for States not to include the exemption method in their treaties. Under that approach, the credit method would be provided for in tax treaties, thereby ensuring the relief of juridical double taxation, and it would be left to domestic law to provide whether that should be done through the credit or exemption method (or probably through a combination of the two methods depending on the nature of the income, as is the case of the domestic law of many countries). The issue that may arise from granting a credit for underlying taxes (which is not a feature of Articles 23 A and 23 B of the OECD Model Tax Convention) is discussed below.

Credit method

141. As regards the application of the credit method provided for by paragraph 2 of Article 23 A and by Article 23 B, the recommendation that relief should be restricted "in proportion to the net taxable income under the arrangement" appears to conform to the domestic tax limitation provided by that method. As noted in paragraphs 60 and 63 of the Commentary on Articles 23 A and 23 B, Article 23 B leaves it to domestic law to determine the domestic tax against which the foreign tax credit should be applied (the "maximum deduction") and one would normally expect that this would be the State of residence's tax as computed after taking into account all relevant deductions:

> *60. Article 23 B sets out the main rules of the credit method, but does not give detailed rules on the computation and operation of the credit. ... Experience has shown that many problems may arise. Some of them are dealt with in the following paragraphs. In many States, detailed rules on credit for foreign tax already exist in their domestic laws. A number of conventions, therefore, contain a reference to the domestic laws of the Contracting States and further provide that such domestic rules shall not affect the principle laid down in Article 23 B.*
>
> *63. The maximum deduction is normally computed as the tax on net income, i.e. on the income from State E (or S) less allowable deductions (specified or proportional) connected with such income...*

142. It is recognised, however, that double non-taxation situations may arise in the application of the credit method by reasons of treaty or domestic law provisions that either supplement, or depart from, the basic approach of Article 23 B (Credit Method) of the OECD Model Tax Convention. One example would be domestic law provisions that allow the foreign tax credit applicable to one item of income to be used against the State of residence's tax payable on another item of income. Another example would be where treaty or domestic law provisions provide for an underlying foreign tax credit with respect to dividends, which may create difficulties with respect to the part of the recommendation on dividend exemption (see paragraph 136) according to which "jurisdictions should consider adopting similar restrictions for other types of dividend relief granted to relieve economic double taxation on underlying profits.". These are other situations where Contracting States should ensure that their tax treaties provide for the elimination of double taxation without creating opportunities for tax avoidance strategies.

Potential application of anti-discrimination provisions in the OECD Model Convention

143. The basic thrust of the recommendations set out in Part I of this Report is to ensure that payments are treated consistently in the hands of the payer and the recipient and, in particular, to prevent a double deduction or deduction without a corresponding inclusion. These recommendations do not appear to raise any issue of discrimination based on nationality (Art. 24(1)). They also do not appear to treat permanent establishments differently from domestic enterprises (Art. 24(3), to provide different rules for the deduction of payments made to residents and non-residents (Art. 24(4)) or to treat domestic enterprises differently based on whether their capital is owned or controlled by residents or non-residents (Art. 24(5)).

144. Some of the domestic law recommendations to neutralise the effects of hybrid mismatch arrangements that are included in Part I may impact payments to non-residents more than they will impact payments to residents. This, however, is not relevant for the purposes of Article 24 as long as the distinction is based on the treatment of the payments in the hands of the payors and recipients. The fact that a mismatch in the tax treatment of an entity or payment is less likely in a purely domestic context (i.e. one would expect a country to be consistent in the way it characterises domestic payments and entities) cannot be interpreted as meaning that rules that are strictly based on the existence of such a mismatch are treating payments to non-residents, or to non-resident owned enterprises, differently from the

way payments to residents, or resident-owned enterprises, are treated under domestic law.

145. The following excerpts from the Commentary on Article 24 are of particular relevance in that context:

- *As regards all the provisions of Art. 24:* "The non-discrimination provisions of the Article seek to balance the need to prevent unjustified discrimination with the need to take account of these legitimate distinctions. For that reason, the Article should not be unduly extended to cover so-called "indirect" discrimination." (paragraph 1)

  "Also, whilst the Article seeks to eliminate distinctions that are solely based on certain grounds, it is not intended to provide foreign nationals, non-residents, enterprises of other States or domestic enterprises owned or controlled by non-residents with a tax treatment that is better than that of nationals, residents or domestic enterprises owned or controlled by residents …" (paragraph 3)

- *As regards Art. 24(3)*: "That principle, therefore, is restricted to a comparison between the rules governing the taxation of the permanent establishment's own activities and those applicable to similar business activities carried on by an independent resident enterprise. It does not extend to rules that take account of the relationship between an enterprise and other enterprises (e.g. rules that allow consolidation, transfer of losses or tax-free transfers of property between companies under common ownership) since the latter rules do not focus on the taxation of an enterprise's own business activities similar to those of the permanent establishment but, instead, on the taxation of a resident enterprise as part of a group of associated enterprises." (paragraph 41)

- *As regards Art 24(4):* "This paragraph is designed to end a particular form of discrimination resulting from the fact that in certain countries the deduction of interest, royalties and other disbursements allowed without restriction when the recipient is resident, is restricted or even prohibited when he is a non-resident." (paragraph 73)

- *As regards Art. 24(5):* "Since the paragraph relates only to the taxation of resident enterprises and not to that of the persons owning or controlling their capital, it follows that it cannot be interpreted to extend the benefits of rules that take account of the relationship between a resident enterprise and other resident enterprises (e.g.

> rules that allow consolidation, transfer of losses or tax-free transfer of property between companies under common ownership)." (paragraph 77)

> "...it follows that withholding tax obligations that are imposed on a resident company with respect to dividends paid to non-resident shareholders but not with respect to dividends paid to resident shareholders cannot be considered to violate paragraph 5. In that case, the different treatment is not dependent on the fact that the capital of the company is owned or controlled by non-residents but, rather, on the fact that dividends paid to non-residents are taxed differently." (paragraph 78)

146. For these reasons, and subject to an analysis of the detailed explanations that will be provided in the proposed commentary and the precise wording of the domestic rules that would be drafted to implement the recommendations the recommendations set out in Part I of this Report would not appear to raise concerns about a possible conflict with the provisions of Article 24 of the OECD Model Tax Convention.

Note

1. "4. The provisions of paragraph 1 [*of Article 23 A*] shall not apply to income derived or capital owned by a resident of a Contracting State where the other Contracting State applies the provisions of this Convention to exempt such income or capital from tax or applies the provisions of paragraph 2 of Article 10 or 11 to such income."

ORGANISATION FOR ECONOMIC CO-OPERATION AND DEVELOPMENT

The OECD is a unique forum where governments work together to address the economic, social and environmental challenges of globalisation. The OECD is also at the forefront of efforts to understand and to help governments respond to new developments and concerns, such as corporate governance, the information economy and the challenges of an ageing population. The Organisation provides a setting where governments can compare policy experiences, seek answers to common problems, identify good practice and work to co-ordinate domestic and international policies.

The OECD member countries are: Australia, Austria, Belgium, Canada, Chile, the Czech Republic, Denmark, Estonia, Finland, France, Germany, Greece, Hungary, Iceland, Ireland, Israel, Italy, Japan, Korea, Luxembourg, Mexico, the Netherlands, New Zealand, Norway, Poland, Portugal, the Slovak Republic, Slovenia, Spain, Sweden, Switzerland, Turkey, the United Kingdom and the United States. The European Union takes part in the work of the OECD.

OECD Publishing disseminates widely the results of the Organisation's statistics gathering and research on economic, social and environmental issues, as well as the conventions, guidelines and standards agreed by its members.

OECD PUBLISHING, 2, rue André-Pascal, 75775 PARIS CEDEX 16
(23 2014 26 1 P) ISBN 978-92-64-21879-6 – 2014